The Minimum Core for Information and Communication Technology:

Knowledge, Understanding and Personal Skills

Achieving **QTLS**

The Minimum Core for
Information and
Communication
Technology:

Knowledge, Understanding and Personal Skills

Alan Clarke

LearningMatters

First published in 2009 by Learning Matters Ltd

British Library Cataloguing in Publication Data
A CIP record for this book is available from the British Library.

ISBN 978 1 84445 269 9

The right of Alan Clarke to be identified as Author of this Work has been asserted by him in accordance with the Copyright, Designs and Patents Act 1988.

Cover design by Topics – The Creative Partnership
Text design by Code 5
Project Management by Deer Park Productions, Tavistock, Devon
Typeset by Pantek Arts Ltd, Maidstone, Kent
Printed and bound in Great Britain by Bell & Bain Ltd, Glasgow

Learning Matters Ltd
33 Southernhay East
Exeter EX1 1NX
Tel: 01392 215560
info@learningmatters.co.uk
www.learningmatters.co.uk

Mixed Sources
Product group from well-managed
forests and other controlled sources
www.fsc.org   Cert no. TT-COC-002769
© 1996 Forest Stewardship Council
FSC

Contents

The author

Dr Alan Clarke is Associate Director for ICT and Learning at the National Institute for Adult Continuing Education (NIACE) and is an Open University teacher. He has been involved with ICT and computer-based learning for over 20 years and is currently a member of the DfES Standards Unit expert group on ICT and the DfES Skill for Life partners group.

Acknowledgements

The author and publisher would like to thank the following for permission to reproduce copyright material: the Institute for Learning; Microsoft product screenshots reprinted with permission from Microsoft Corporation; screenshots reprinted with permission from Google.

Every effort has been made to trace the copyright holders and to obtain permission for the use of copyright material. The publisher and author will gladly receive any information enabling them to rectify any error or omission in subsequent editions.

List of acronyms

ACL   Adult and community learning

ATLS   Associate Teacher Learning and Skills

CPD   continuous professional development

CTLLS   Certificate in teaching in the lifelong learning sector

DDA   Disability and Discrimination Act

DfES   Department for Education and Skills

DTLLS   Diploma in teaching in the lifelong learning sector

DVLA   Driver and Vehicle Licensing Agency

FE   further education

ICT   information and communication technology

ILT   information and learning technology

LLUK   Lifelong Learning UK

LSIS   Learning and Skills Improvement Service

OLAS   offender learning and skills

QTLS   Qualified Teacher Learning and Skills

RSC   Regional Support Centre

RSI   repetitive strain injury

SENDA   Special Education Needs and Disability Act

VLA   virtual learning environment

WBL   work-based learning

Introduction

Information and Communication Technology (ICT) was made a skill for life or a basic skill in 2003 alongside literacy and numeracy in the White Paper, *21st Century Skills: Realising Our Potential*. This recognised that ICT is an essential part of the economy and society. ICT skills are now required by the majority of new jobs (Leitch, 2005). Equally, technology has become a key factor in society as a whole with an ever-increasing use of online communication to undertake daily tasks (e.g. checking train timetables, shopping for food, completing income tax returns and taxing your car). However, many people still do not use ICT. The *Delivering Digital Inclusion* consultation document (HM Government, 2008) states that there are 17 million people over the age of 15 not using the internet or computers. The document makes the point that there is a strong correlation between being digitally excluded and socially excluded, with six million people in both categories. E-learning in all its forms is growing rapidly so that the curriculum, learning methods and administration all require learners to have some degree of ICT skills in order to cope with the demands of their course. ICT joined literacy and numeracy as a requirement of the Minimum Core in 2007 demonstrating its importance as a skill that adults needed to function in the modern work.

As a new or trainee teacher you need to be are aware of the ICT needs of your learners so that you can teach your subjects as effectively as possible. Learners need the help and assistance of their teachers to progress. Many will not want to take a specialist course in ICT but would rather learn the skills in another context. Some learners will have had a poor experience of studying ICT and will be seeking to progress their education through an alternative route which may be in a formal or an informal setting.

This book is aimed not only at new teachers but also at experienced ones who are seeking to continue their professional development. It will help with your own personal skills in this area as well as helping you support your learners. The opening chapter enables you to undertake a knowledge and skills assessment and develop an action plan to help you realise your professional objectives. The book follows the structure of the ICT minimum core's knowledge, understanding and personal skills.

The titles of each chapter relate directly to the knowledge, understanding and personal skills needed by tutors identified in LLUK (2007). Each chapter opens with a set of objectives which identify the learning outcomes of the chapter and are linked directly to the ICT minimum core. The links to professional standards identified in LLUK (n.d.) and to the Certificate (CTLLS) and Diploma (DTLLS) in teaching in the lifelong learning sector qualifications are shown. The book should also be helpful to people studying for the Certificate or Post/Professional Graduate Certificate in Education.

ICT is both a curriculum subject and a means of supporting and delivering learning. It could therefore be argued that the book has a general relationship across all the certificate and diploma units. The book contents should assist you to use e-learning methods more appropriately and help identify the barriers that some learners will encounter.

Each chapter offers scenarios, practical and reflective tasks that are based on real-life experience and provide a context for the work. At the end of each chapter there is a short summary of the key points and a list of the references used and suggestions for further reading. This is not an exhaustive list of sources and there are many others that you will identify as well.

REFERENCES AND FURTHER READING REFERENCES AND FURTHER READING

HM Government (2008) *Delivering Digital Inclusion: An Action Plan for Consultation, Communities and Local Government*. London: HM Government.

Leitch, (2005) *Review of Skills* [online]. Available at: www.hm-treasury.gov.uk/4027.htm [accessed 15 October 2008].

LLUK (2007) *Addressing literacy, language, numeracy and ICT needs in education and training: Defining the minimum core of teachers' knowledge, understanding and personal skills*. London: Lifelong Learning UK.

LLUK (nd) *New overarching professional standards for teachers, tutors and trainers in the lifelong learning sector*. London: Lifelong Learning UK.

1
Your professional development

This chapter will help you to:

- **understand the Continuous Professional Development (CPD) process;**
- **undertake a personal knowledge and skills assessment for ICT;**
- **identify an action plan for your development;**
- **understand how to record evidence of your development.**

Links to minimum core ICT
A2   Develop your personal ICT skills and knowledge and reflect upon your own experiences.
       However, this chapter relates to the whole ICT minimum core so that there is a relation-
       ship to the whole standard.

Links to LLUK Professional Standards
AS4   Reflection and evaluation of your own practice and your own continuing professional
       development as teachers.
AS7   Improving the quality of your practice.

Links to Diploma in Teaching in the Lifelong Learning Sector (DTLLS)
Unit 5 Continuing personal and professional development.

Introduction

It is not enough to become a qualified teacher or trainer in the further education (FE) sector. You need to maintain and enhance your skills and understanding through a process of CPD throughout your career. Since September 2007 full-time teachers and trainers in the FE sector have been required to carry out a minimum of 30 hours of CPD each year and part-time staff a pro rata amount. They must also record their development activities. In the context of this book, CPD means to keep up to date with the contents of the ICT minimum core. ICT is a dynamic and rapidly changing subject. Its impact on society and specifically on education and training is developing quickly so there is an on going need to maintain and extend your skills and knowledge. CPD is essential if you are not to fall behind.

The aims of the ICT minimum core (LLUK, 2007b) are:

- to promote an understanding that underpinning ICT skills may be necessary for learners to succeed and achieve their chosen qualification;
- to encourage the development of inclusive practices in addressing the ICT needs of learners;
- to raise awareness of the benefits to learners of developing embedded approaches to teaching and learning the Skills for Life;
- to provide signposts to useful materials that will support collaborative working with specialist ICT teachers in understanding how to integrate these skills within other areas of specialism.

The Institute for Learning (2007) offers the dual model of CPD that asks teachers to consider not only their subject but also teaching and learning and the policy context in which they are working. You need to balance your CPD across the three areas. In some cases the emphasis may be on some areas more than others.

The ICT minimum core requires that teachers are able to support learners with limited ICT skills. This may have an impact on all three areas of the dual model.

For example:

ICT may form part of your subject specialism.

E-learning methods may be used during the course that assume a level of learner skill (e.g. searching the world wide web).

Government policy may require actions by the education or training provider in relation to ICT (e.g. HM Goverment, 2008).

The Institute for Learning provides a model for the CPD process. Figure 1.1 shows the model. This requires a systematic and objective approach in which you need to analyse your skills and knowledge in relation to your objectives. This analysis provides the basis of your development or action plan. The activities identified within the plan are undertaken and recorded. The final step is to reflect on what you have achieved and feed the conclusions into the next cycle of the CPD process.

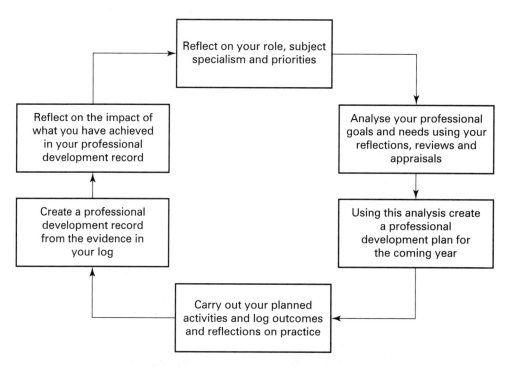

Figure 1.1 Institute for Learning CPD process model

Reflection

Reflection is a major component of the Institute for Learning's CPD process and forms a key element in the requirements for many other professions. In addition it can help you to achieve deep learning. Undertake the following reflective tasks.

REFLECTIVE TASK

1 Consider how ICT is changing your teaching subject. How will you need to adapt your approach to meet the changes and assist your learners?

2 Consider how ICT is changing society, the world of work and people's lives. How will you need to adapt your approach to meet the changes and assist your learners?

3 Consider how ICT is changing teaching and learning. How will you need to adapt your approach to meet the changes and assist your learners?

CASE STUDY – JUNE

June is an experienced local history teacher with many years' experience of working with adult learners who undertake the course. The learners are often over 50 years old and many have retired from full-time employment. However, some are younger and are of the opinion that the possibilities the internet offers for finding information and for learners to communicate with each other between sessions should be part of the course. She is not sure how to achieve this outcome even though she is convinced they are right. The college has good facilities to allow the students access to the internet as well as video projectors and electronic whiteboards. Everyone is allocated an e-mail address but many of her students never use it. However, she has doubts about her own skills and also how to manage the classroom. How can she help the learners to develop the necessary skills?

Discussion

There are several ways of solving this problem. Three actions seem appropriate:

1. Prioritise and integrate the changes into the curriculum – plan an exercise such as using a video projector to show a key website so that you can demonstrate how to browse and what to look for. This exercise can be planned in advance and practiced so that it is effective.
2. Use the resources of computer literate and enthusiastic learners to support the others. This will take a lot of the burden off you as learners often respond well to peer support. Once the initial exercise is complete, divide the class into groups and ask them as a team to undertake a search for specific information.
3. Investigate what support the college provides to help teachers when using e-learning approaches. Many colleges and other providers have e-learning (sometimes called Information and Learning Technology or ILT) champions or e-guides who have a role in assisting colleagues to develop their skills and knowledge.

ICT minimum core analysis

Table 1.1 provides a means of analysing your understanding and skills in relation to the ICT minimum core. The columns ICT minimum core areas and Key areas present a short version of the standard. You may also find it useful to consider the full standard which is available from the Lifelong Learning UK website. In the Understanding and skills column indicate your current knowledge and skills and in the Activity column those actions that could help you develop your skills in that area. The final step is to use the last column, Priority, to show how important that area is to your development.

Each chapter of the book relates directly to the standard so you may find it useful to review the summaries at the ends of the chapters. This will possibly help you decide on relevance and importance.

PRACTICAL TASK PRACTICAL TASK PRACTICAL TASK PRACTICAL TASK PRACTICAL TASK

Analysis

The ICT minimum core analysis table displays the contents of the standard. Each main section relates to a chapter of the book. Consider each section and judge your knowledge and skills in that area, identify any activities that would help you develop your skills and knowledge and finally prioritise the area. Use the reflections that you have undertaken earlier plus any feedback that you have received from reviews and appraisals. Complete the table.

ICT minimum core areas	Key areas	Understanding and skills	Activity	Priority
Different factors affecting the acquisition and development of ICT skills	be aware of a range of personal and social factors			
	be able to reflect on your own and learners' attitudes and attainment			
	be aware of ICT research in the acquisition and development of ICT skills			
Importance of ICT in enabling users to participate in public life, society and the modern economy	understand the importance of ICT in enabling users to participate in and gain access to society			
	understand the importance of ICT in enabling users to participate in and gain access to the modern economy			
Main learning disabilities and difficulties relating to ICT learning and skill development	be aware of the impact that learning difficulties and disabilities, as described in *Delivering Skills for Life: Introducing Access for All*, can have on ICT learning			

Table 1.1 ICT minimum core analysis

ICT minimum core areas	Key areas	Understanding and skills	Activity	Priority
	be supportive of strategies that learners can use to overcome difficulties in their ICT use and learning			
	be aware of the resources, specialist equipment, teaching strategies and referral procedures that can help learners overcome their difficulties in ICT use and learning			
Potential barriers that inhibit ICT skills development	be aware of personal factors that may inhibit the development of ICT skills			
	be aware of the institutional factors that may inhibit the development of ICT skills			
	be aware of the teaching and learning factors that may inhibit the development of ICT skills			
Communicating about ICT	be aware of methods and purposes of assessment in ICT			
	be aware of the role of communication in ICT			
	be aware of effective ways to communicate			
	understand what is meant by purposeful use of ICT			
	understand the essential characteristics of ICT			
	be aware of the ways learners develop ICT skills			

Table 1.1 ICT minimum core analysis

ICT minimum core areas	Key areas	Understanding and skills	Activity	Priority
Personal ICT Skills – Communication	communicate with/about ICT in a manner that supports open discussion			
	be able to assess your own, and others' understanding			
	be able to recognise differences in language needs; formulate and provide appropriate responses and recognise appropriate use of communication about/ with ICT by others			
	be able to use language and other forms of representation			
Personal ICT Skills – Processes	use ICT Systems			
	find, select and exchange information			
	develop and present information			

Table 1.1 ICT minimum core analysis

Development action plan

There are various ways of constructing and organising a continuous professional development action plan. The Institute for Learning provides an e-portfolio system called Reflect which is based on a commercial product called PebblePad. This offers the means to create an action plan that includes:

- describing your current position;
- identifying your objectives;
- describing the development process you plan to undertake;
- analysing your strengths and weaknesses;
- identifying resources to assist with your learning (e.g. books, people, courses etc.);
- the opportunity to reflect.

You can share your action plan with colleagues, managers and friends. It is often helpful to ask for feedback which can lead to improving your plan.

Current position

The key to an effective plan is knowing what your current skills and knowledge are so that you can judge the progress that you will make. Assess yourself, then ask managers and colleagues for their views and record them. The ICT minimum core analysis table will help you systematically assess your position.

Objectives

Develop some realistic objectives for yourself that are SMART, that is:

- **S**pecific – ones that clearly specify what you aim to achieve;
- **M**easurable – so you can judge that they have been achieved;
- **A**chievable – objectives that are possible;
- **R**ealistic – sensible within the limits of the time and other resources available to you;
- **T**ime – how long do you need to achieve your objectives?

Process

How are you going to achieve your objectives? In this section you will need to consider systematically each step that you will need to take.

For example:

> Step 1: Read *Inclusive learning approaches for literacy, language, numeracy and ICT* (LLUK, 2007a), so that I gain a clear understanding of the ICT minimum core by January.
> Step 2: Discuss with ICT specialist staff the most appropriate ways of supporting learners with poor ICT skills by March.

It is important to be realistic, giving yourself adequate time and other resources to carry out the process. You should not overestimate what you can achieve in a given period of time. It can be very de-motivating to fall behind. Identify any opportunities or barriers to carrying out the development plan.

REFLECTIVE TASK

If you have undertaken professional development consider your experience and identify what were the most effective practices that you had and why.

Resources

CPD is not simply about going on courses but rather any activity that will help you develop your skills and knowledge. Resources are anything that can assist your development such as:

- observing colleagues;
- reading books;
- discussions with peers;
- browsing websites.

The Institute for Learning's publication *Guidelines for CPD* (2007) provides guidance on CPD activities in the three areas of specialism, policy and teaching and learning.

PRACTICAL TASK PRACTICAL TASK PRACTICAL TASK PRACTICAL TASK PRACTICAL TASK

Development plan ICT minimum core

Using the outcomes of your analysis, construct an action plan in which you identify your objectives with respect to the ICT minimum core. Consider how you can achieve each objective and what resources you will need. It is important to be realistic about what you can achieve in a given time period. Once you have a written plan, ask a colleague to review it and provide you with feedback.

PRACTICAL TASK PRACTICAL TASK PRACTICAL TASK PRACTICAL TASK PRACTICAL TASK

Development plan ICT minimum core – alternative

If you are a member of the Institute for Learning use the Reflect e-portfolio to create an action plan.

Record

Teachers and trainers in the FE and Skills sector are required to record their development activities. This is in order to show that they are maintaining their professional skills and understanding. You need to keep records of your activities. The Institute for Learning requires that you complete a statement of completed CPD on a standard form each year. On this form you need to specify where the Institute can access your records should they select it to audit. The Institute offers members access to an e-portfolio system designed to store records. This is called Reflect.

Reflect provides a sophisticated e-portfolio system whereby you can: create action plans, record experience, upload files, share your records with other people to gain feedback and select content to present to others, as well as other activities.

Records of evidence can take a variety of forms but three items are worth highlighting. They are:

1. your own reflections on your experiences; reflection is a vital element in achieving deep learning and is part of every professional's skill set;
2. feedback from your learners that enables you to improve your practice;
3. discussions with your peers about your professional practice – this may form a part of your reflective process since a colleague can offer constructive feedback on both your plans and activities.

PRACTICAL TASK PRACTICAL TASK PRACTICAL TASK PRACTICAL TASK PRACTICAL TASK

Evidence

Review a CPD activity that you have undertaken and consider what would be appropriate evidence to demonstrate your development. Develop the evidence and record it.

CASE STUDY – ANDREW

Andrew is a new FE GCSE English teacher who is preparing to teach a group of 16-year-old students. He has been told by his colleagues that the college expects all teachers to use technology as much as possible to enhance learning and that young people are very skilled in using technology. However, he is not sure how to begin to prepare for the new course. His own ICT skills are good and he has attended a course on e-learning as part of his training.

Discussion

Starting is often difficult for many teachers and trainers. In this case there are a variety of possible steps but some are:

1. Identify what facilities the college can provide you. They may have a Virtual Learning Environment (VLE) with discussion forums that will allow you and the learners to communicate with each other between sessions.
2. Identify which classrooms you will be working in since facilities may vary between rooms.
3. Consider the curriculum for the course and how suitable it is for an e-learning approach (e.g. information required, group projects, multimedia creation etc.). E-learning has strengths and weaknesses and different topics may need different approaches.
4. Find out more about the group. It is a generalisation to say that all 16-year-olds will be expert users of ICT. They will have different levels of skill. Disadvantaged young people often have had no access to ICT at home so their skills are not as advanced as those of others in the group. However, they may have attended schools in which electronic whiteboards were regularly used, so they will come with some expectations.
5. Advanced ICT skills do not mean that students are skilled learners. Young people may have limited or even poor study skills and online learning requires a different mix of learning skills than traditional methods (Clarke, 2008).
6. Students' attitudes to using technology in their education are complex. A recent research report (Ipsos Mori, 2007) that focused on undergraduate students shows that not everyone is enthusiastic about different technologies or applications.

A SUMMARY OF KEY POINTS

> All full-time teachers and trainers have been required since September 2007 to carry out a minimum of 30 hours of CPD each year and part-time staff a pro rata amount. They are also required to record their development activities.

> The Institute for Learning (2007) offers the dual model of CPD that asks teachers to consider not only their subject but also teaching and learning and the policy context in which they are working.

> The Institute for Learning provides a model (Figure 1.1) for the CPD process.

> Reflection is a key component of CPD process.

> Assessment of your current skills and knowledge is a key component in developing a CPD action plan.

> The Institute for Learning provides an e-portfolio system called Reflect that offers the means to create a CPD action plan.

> An action plan needs to contain objectives, process, resources and records.

> Teachers and trainers in the FE and Skills sector are required to record their development activities.

REFERENCES AND FURTHER READING REFERENCES AND FURTHER READING

Clarke, A (2008) *E-learning Skills,* Second Edition. Basingstoke: Palgrave Macmillan.

DfES (nd) *Delivering Skills for Life: Introducing Access for All*. London: DfES.

HM Government (2008) *Delivering Digital Inclusion: An Action Plan for Consultation, Communities and Local Government.* London: HM Goverment.

Institute for Learning (2007) *Guidelines for your continuing professional development (CPD)* [online]. Available at: www.ifl.ac.uk/services/p_wwv_page?id=171&menu_id=1340 [accessed 13 November 2008].

Ipsos Mori (2007), *Student Expectation Study* [online]. Available at: Available at: www.jisc.ac.uk/publications/publications/studentexpectations.aspx#downloads [accessed November 2008].

Leitch, *Review of Skills* www.hm-treasury.gov.uk/4027.htm [accessed 15 October 2008].

LLUK (2007a) *Inclusive learning approaches for literacy, language, numeracy and ICT*. London: Lifelong Learning UK.

LLUK (2007b) *Addressing literacy, language, numeracy and ICT needs in education and training: Defining the minimum core of teachers' knowledge, understanding and personal skills*. London: Lifelong Learning UK.

LLUK (nd) *New overarching professional standards for teachers, tutors and trainers in the lifelong learning sector.* London: Lifelong Learning UK.

2
Different factors affecting the acquisition and development of ICT skills

This chapter will help you to:

- be aware of a range of personal and social factors, including attitudes in the wider society, age, motivation, gender, socio-economic status, ethnicity and disability or learning difficulty that affect the acquisition and development of ICT skills;
- be able to reflect on your own and learners' attitudes and attainment, with regard to personal use and new learning that involves ICT;
- be aware of ICT research in the acquisition and development of ICT skills.

Links to minimum core ICT
A1   Awareness of a range of personal and social factors, including attitudes in the wider society, age, motivation, gender, socio-economic status, ethnicity and disability or learning difficulty that affect the acquisition and development of ICT skills.

Links to LLUK Professional Standards
AK1.1 What motivates learners to learn and the importance of learners' experience and aspirations.
AK3.1 Issues of equality, diversity and inclusion.

Links to Certificate in Teaching in the Lifelong Learning Sector (CTLLS)
Unit 2 Planning and enabling learning.

Links to Diploma in Teaching in the Lifelong Learning Sector (DTLLS)
Unit 2 Planning and enabling learning.
Unit 4 Theories and principles for planning and enabling learning.

Introduction

Each year, hundreds of thousands of people undertake ICT education and training courses, indicating the importance of technology to individuals and organisations. For many organisations ICT is now a vital factor in their operation so that the technology skills, attitudes and knowledge of their staff are critical. E-mail dominates company communication, word processing is universally used by administration staff and databases of customers are often vital to the success of the business.

Government has made considerable investments in online services, demonstrating their commitment to ICT as a means of communicating with citizens. The majority of Members of Parliament have e-mail addresses and websites and many utilise blogs to influence their constituents. Local authorities provide information about their services via websites and provide access to the internet through terminals in libraries. People's everyday lives are now integrated with technology with online shopping, online recruitment, digital cameras, planning journeys using websites, helping their children with their education and numerous other activities that come with ICT. All educational sectors are now employing e-learning. Online courses in a wide range of subjects are available from many colleges and universities. Technology is now a key part in all areas of society.

The change that technology has brought about continues to accelerate so that the level of ICT skills we require to function is becoming increasingly more advanced. Many employers have identified the need for employees to have higher level skills (Gartner, 2004; e-skills, 2008). In order to take advantage of the opportunities that ICT will increasingly provide and to continue to participate in society requires that users are able to enhance their skills and knowledge and adapt to new situations. This means that for new ICT users the initial steps are becoming increasingly higher. A Department for Education and Skills (DfES) survey in 2003 showed that 53 per cent of adults had very limited ICT practical skills.

There have been many surveys and investigations that have considered the motivation of people to develop ICT skills and knowledge. These include (Prime Minister's Strategy Unit, 2005; HM Government, 2008):

- employment (i.e. increased income);
- supporting learners' learning;
- supporting the education of learners' children;
- accessing government online services (e.g. Inland Revenue Self Assessment);
- shopping online;
- assistive technology for disabled people;
- communication with family and friends;
- hobbies and interests (e.g. digital photography);
- finding information, advice and services.

Individual users will have their own mix of needs and these must be considered when providing education and training programmes.

REFLECTIVE TASK

Reflect on your own initial reasons for learning ICT skills and knowledge and consider if they have changed. What are your motives now for learning about ICT?

The surveys and investigations have also identified the reasons people give for not learning about ICT. They include:

- cannot see the relevance of technology to themselves;
- cannot identify the benefits of technology to themselves;
- lack confidence in their ability to learn about technology;
- have concerns about security of technology;
- have concerns about unsuitable content on the internet .

Several researchers (Digital Inclusion Panel, 2004; Selwyn, 2002) have concluded that individuals need their own 'compelling proposition' to motivate them to learn about ICT. These are personal reasons that provide a powerful stimulus to learning that overcomes the negative factors such as a lack of confidence in their own abilities. The education or training approach needs to satisfy the learners' needs.

Benefits

Delivering Digital Inclusion (2008) and other publications (Clarke, 2006, 2008) have identified a range of benefits that ICT can bring for particular groups of individuals and
communities. They include:

- learning at their own pace, place and time;
- economic – increased income and assistance with recruitment;
- access to information, advice and guidance (e.g. social networks);
- overcoming some of the barriers that disabled people encounter;
- preventing re-offending;
- supporting older people to continue to live independently and be socially engaged;
- assisting with consulting communities;
- supporting rural communities;
- helping communities become more sustainable.

PRACTICAL TASK PRACTICAL TASK PRACTICAL TASK PRACTICAL TASK PRACTICAL TASK

Consider the above benefits and decide which one is most appropriate to the subject that you teach. How
could you integrate it into your teaching?

ICT education and training

The approach taken to provide ICT skills and knowledge courses has often been based
on the workshop in which each individual learner works on tasks provided by the tutor.
The tasks are aimed mainly at helping the learner to be able to use a range of applications (e.g. word processing, spreadsheets and databases). It is also characterised by
relatively poor retention and achievement rates compared to other subjects. NIACE
(2005) and Luger (2007) reported that existing ICT education and training practice tends
to be:

- focused on a relatively narrow range of methods (e.g. the worksheet);
- concentrated around applications;
- general rather than meeting specific individual needs.

These approaches are probably effective if the learners are self-confident and have a
preference for learning on their own. It is probably not very effective if learners lack confidence or have preferences for more collaborative approaches. Clarke (2006) in
Teaching Adults ICT Skills showed that a wide range of teaching and learning methods
could be employed, such as peer support, group activities and whole class teaching.
This richer approach to the teaching and learning of ICT is important considering:

- the dynamic and changing nature of ICT that will require skills and knowledge to be
  updated continuously;
- the need to be able to transfer skills to new situations as technology develops into
  different forms and approaches;
- the need to employ technology in many contexts (e.g. work, leisure, community,
  society and learning);
- the need for the initial learning experience to provide a sound foundation for future
  development.

REFLECTIVE TASK

Reflect on how you have learnt ICT skills and decide what were the most effective ways and why.

Many socially or economically disadvantaged adults have had poor experiences of education so are not well motivated to take part in learning in institutional locations. However, they are often willing to undertake learning in familiar community locations. ICT courses have been delivered in community settings for many years as part of outreach programmes or in local UK Online centres. A series of evaluation and research reports (Clarke et al, 2003; Ipsos Mori, 2008) have shown that ICT courses are often effective in building confidence and improving the self-esteem of disadvantaged learners. They are often prepared to progress onto other courses of study after the initial experience.

Between Janurary 2007 and 2008, 20 Social Impact Demonstrator projects were provided through UK Online centres (Ipsos Mori, 2008). They were aimed at engaging disadvantaged people and helping them access the Internet for the first time. The key question was whether through developing ICT skills participants also gained social skills. The project outcomes showed that people grew in self-confidence, developed positive attitudes towards technology from an initial position of frustration and concern with ICT and at the end of the project 85 per cent of participants were using ICT every day.

Case Study – Francis

Francis is an experienced tutor who has been asked to deliver an employability course at a UK Online centre based in a local community. The centre can provide access to computers, the internet and modern application software. Francis would like to integrate ICT into the course but has been told that many of the learners will not have good ICT skills and may also be apprehensive about using the technology. He is not sure how to plan the course.

Discussion

This is a daunting task if you have little experience of working in a community setting. However, it can be a rewarding experience helping people to learn who have little confidence in their own abilities.

1. UK Online centres have enormous experience of helping disadvantaged people to learn to use ICT so it would be useful to consult them. They can advise what materials and other support they have available. They may well have already supported some of your learners so their skills may be more advanced than you anticipate.
2. Although disadvantaged adults often doubt their ability to learn, a few small successes can make a big difference to their self-confidence.
3. The key is to help them succeed in the early stages of the course. This can motivate them to keep coming.
4. Learners are often curious about ICT and this will motivate them to participate, so learning through and about ICT is a positive step.

Embedding

ICT is essentially a set of tools that allow you to undertake a wide variety of tasks. It is therefore suitable to be embedded into other subjects. This has been widely discussed in the context of helping adults to develop their literacy skills. ICT is seen as a motivating factor in encouraging adults to attend literacy programmes. Many adults are motivated to learn through and about ICT. This is partially affected by the stigma attached to literacy while there is little stigma in admitting a lack of technology skills. It is widely reported that one benefit of incorporating technology into learning programmes is that learners improve their ICT skills.

Non-users

Three factors about non-users of technology are clear. These are age, socio-economic status and educational background. Communities and Local Government (2008) analysed the evidence of digital exclusion and concluded that people with no access to the internet were:

- likely to be over 65 years old (just over half of the group);
- in the lowest socio-economic class (DE) (about half of them);
- hold no qualifications higher than secondary school standard (two thirds of them).

However, this simple image is not the whole story. People over 65 years old who do access the internet tend to do so more than other younger users. The use of ICT in the workplace has grown fastest among older workers (over 55 years old) than in any other group since 2001 and now stands at 72 per cent (e-skills, 2008). The proportion of ICT professionals over 40 years old has risen from 32 to 45 per cent over the last six years. This demonstrates that the image of a youthful ICT professional is changing.

Sabates (2007) analysed the access to and use of ICT by 14 year olds. He showed that young socially disadvantaged people often do not have home access and frequently do not or are unable to take full advantage of school technology. The government is so concerned with this lack of home access that they have launched the Home Access programme to address the problem. The National Office of Statistics reported (2007) that 10 per cent of 16 to 24 year olds had not accessed the internet in the three months prior to their survey. This indicates that the popular view that all young people are expert users is misplaced.

Net generation

The net generation is a term used to identify the young people who have grown up in a society where ICT is seen as a normal part of everyday life and education. It is often used to suggest that all young people are competent and confident users of technology. The reality is, in fact, more complex with varying skills and experience. It is wrong to assume that all young people will be confident and competent users of all forms of technology.

Motivation

The National Office of Statistics survey of Internet use (2007) showed that some of the most popular activities were:

- finding information about goods or services (86 per cent);
- sending/receiving e-mails (85 per cent);

- using services related to travel and accommodation (63 per cent);
- obtaining information from public authorities' web sites (46 per cent);
- looking for information about education, training or courses (36 per cent);
- reading or downloading online news, magazines, etc (30 per cent);
- consulting the internet for the purpose of learning (33 per cent);
- looking for a job or sending a job application (21 per cent);
- selling of goods or services (e.g. via auctions) (17 per cent);
- doing an online course (in any subject) (6 per cent).

The list indicates the motivation of internet users. A further factor in considering motivation is that home (87 per cent) and work (44 per cent) are the most likely place to use the internet. An educational location is used by only 12 per cent to access the internet. Users often use the internet from home, friends' houses or from work. Many of their online activities are related to their social, family or work lives.

If these activities motivate users then they are also likely to serve as reasons for non-users to become interested in learning ICT skills. Several researchers have indicated the key to motivating non-users to learn about ICT is realisation what the benefits are for them. The Ipsos Mori research in 2008 identified the following expectations of using computers from learners drawn from socially disadvantaged people:

- keeping up to date (55 per cent);
- confidence building (50 per cent);
- communicating with family and friends (47 per cent);
- achieving new qualifications (31 per cent);
- meeting new people (24 per cent);
- finding a job (22 per cent);
- help with literacy and numeracy (14 per cent);
- finances (9 per cent).

REFLECTIVE TASK

ICT expectations

Consider your own reasons for using ICT. What are your personal expectations? Reflect on these expectations and how they could influence your attitude to ICT.

PRACTICAL TASK PRACTICAL TASK PRACTICAL TASK PRACTICAL TASK PRACTICAL TASK

Ask your learners what are their reasons and expectations for using ICT and the internet. Consider their answers and identify activities within your own teaching in to which you could integrate this type of task.

Acquisition and development of ICT skills

Many ICT users have developed their skills through their own efforts either by trial and error or through using self study material. The National Office of Statistics survey of internet use (2007) reported that 51 per cent learnt by doing and 17 per cent through self-study resources. In addition, many people sought help from friends or colleagues. A minority of users attended education and training courses. The Oxford Internet Survey (Dutton and Helsper, 2007) reported that only 21 per cent of users attended training courses compared to 78 per cent who worked things out for themselves.

This interest in trying to solve problems and explore technology has been linked to the ICT Skill for Life standard's emphasis on purposefulness, that is, providing courses that offer learners the opportunity to learn about ICT in a context that is appropriate to them. The traditional method has often been to concentrate on assisting learners to become skilled in using the main applications such as word processing, spreadsheets and databases. This has sometimes resulted in an almost context-free environment so learners can sometimes fail to see what the relevance of an application is to their needs. The ICT Skill for Life standard adopts a more context and purposeful approach to make the courses more relevant to the learners. The ICT National Vocational Qualification is the ITQ, which has an interesting structure in that learners can select from a range of modules at different levels. The learners can customise the programme to meet their needs to some extent.

ICT is continuously changing and extending with new operating systems and applications appearing all the time. There is also the probability that learners will encounter different versions of applications as they change employment, use public systems or simply travel to new locations. This means that learners need to be always developing their skills and coping with different versions of applications and systems. In other words, they need to be able to transfer their learning to new situations and products if they are to cope with the different ICT environments they encounter. This requires more than simple rote learning of applications. Learners need to understand the structure of the applications and the internet.

If they have not been prepared new ICT learners often find it very confusing when they encounter a different version of an application. It is good practice to show learners a range of versions and to indicate the common elements between them to help them transfer their understanding. Courses can often treat each application separately without explaining that they share many functions. For example, by understanding saving, printing, copying a file and many other functions in one Microsoft Office application you can do it in all of them. The ICT Functional Skills standards (QCA, 2007) state that *For ICT to be useful, learners must have the skills and confidence to apply, combine and adapt their ICT knowledge to new situations in their life and work.*

A vital component of developing ICT skills is practice so learners are often encouraged to work on exercises between formal sessions. Many ICT tutors provide materials for personal study. There are also a variety of books aimed at students to help them develop their skills and understanding. Many colleges, UK Online centres and libraries offer drop-in facilities to allow learners to practise their skills.

Many conventional ICT courses are built around a workshop approach in which learners use worksheets that allow them to progress at their own pace. This tends to be appropriate for learners who prefer this type of learning style. However, to meet the full range of learners' needs, it is appropriate to use a wider range of methods such as small group tasks, peer support, demonstrations and whole-class activities. These would enrich the course and achieve better results. It is useful when teaching ICT to blend this range of methods with workshop activities and practice (Clarke, 2006).

PRACTICAL TASK PRACTICAL TASK PRACTICAL TASK PRACTICAL TASK PRACTICAL TASK

Learners

Ask your learners how they prefer to learn about ICT. What have they found to be the most and least effective methods and why?

CASE STUDY – ALICE

Alice is a Business Studies teacher who is aware that many of the employers with whom she has communicated stress the importance of ICT skills in the use of spreadsheets to model financial data. The learners who undertake Business Studies courses are confident users of technology especially the internet, e-mail and social networks but have rarely used spreadsheets. All the learners take part in ICT courses but she is unaware of the details of the curriculum they undertake.

Alice would like to introduce some practical financial exercises that would enhance her courses but she is not sure that she has the skills to support a group who do not have the required ICT skills.

Discussion

There are several ways of addressing this issue but one is:

Discuss the issue with the ICT teachers who provide the learners' courses to clarify what aspects of using spreadsheets they will cover and when. This will allow you to offer exercises that will not only help them develop financial skills but will also provide opportunities to practise their spreadsheet skills.

The opportunity to discuss the different courses may also help in identifying other areas to help learners through co-ordination of the programmes.

Reflection

Reflection is a key skill for professionals in many occupations. The ability to consider your experiences, analyse and identify lessons for the future is vital. It is the route to deep learning and benefiting from experience. ICT is a dynamic and continuously developing area so it is important to be able to adapt and change. This requires a positive attitude to technology and a willingness to explore its potential. As a teacher, you need to see how e-learning methods might assist your teaching, ensure your personal skills are up-to-date and be aware of how your students are using technology.

The Joint Information Services Committee (JISC, 2007) has been supporting a range of research projects to consider the views of higher education students of using technology in their education. These indicate that students own and use a lot of personal technology such as mobile phones, laptops, social network sites and mp3 players. They expect to be able to use these for learning and anticipate teachers supporting their employment. However, there were different needs, with some students requiring help with technology. A quote from the JISC report gives a clear view of the future. *Learners of all ages are developing new working practices around the technologies available to them*. The teacher needs to be aware of this trend and be working to take advantage of these new practices.

You need to reflect on your experiences of technology, how learners are utilising it and identify what you need to do. Figure 2.1 shows the Kolb Cycle which provides a model for development. Concrete experience could consist of observing, doing, undertaking tasks and using ICT applications. This provides the foundation on which reflection can be based. Reflective observation involves reviewing and thinking through the experience to consider what can be learnt from it. Abstract conceptualisation aims to build on experience and the reflection to decide what to do next. Active experimentation allows you to explore new ideas and approaches. This is the step that enables you to investigate the new approach which leads to the start of the cycle again.

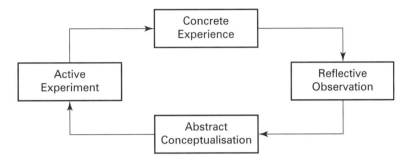

Figure 2.1 ICT reflections

PRACTICAL TASK PRACTICAL TASK PRACTICAL TASK PRACTICAL TASK PRACTICAL TASK

Experiment

Try a new technology approach such as participating in a social network, contributing to a blog, using an e-portfolio or integrating an electronic whiteboard in your teaching. Reflect on the experience and working through the Kolb model, decide how the experience will influence your teaching.

A SUMMARY OF KEY POINTS

> ICT is now vital to all types of organisation including commercial companies, parliament, education and government. Many employers have already identified the need for employees to have higher level skills.

> 53 per cent of adults had very limited ICT practical skills (DfES, 2003).

> Individual learners will have their own mix of needs to motivate them to learn ICT skills.

> Surveys and investigations have identified the reasons that people give for not learning about ICT (e.g. cannot see the relevance of technology to themselves).

> Existing ICT education and training practice has been criticised as using a narrow range of methods, focused on learning to use applications and not meeting individual needs.

> ICT is a dynamic subject. It requires skills and knowledge to be continuously updated, transferable skills and the ability to employ technology in many contexts. It thus needs a mix of methods (e.g. peer support, group activities and whole-class teaching).

> Developing ICT skills can help improve the self-confidence and positive attitudes towards technology of socially disadvantaged learners.

> Non-users are likely to be over 65 years old (just over half of the group), in the lowest socio-economic class (DE) (about half of them) and hold no qualifications higher than secondary school standard (two thirds of them). Equally, socially disadvantaged, underprivileged young people are also more disadvantaged in terms of ICT than their peers.

> The National Office of Statistics survey (2007) identified the most popular uses of the internet.

> The Ipsos Mori research in 2008 identified the expectations of using computers from socially disadvantaged learners.

> Trial and error, self-study and help from friends and colleagues are widely used to develop ICT skills.

> The ICT Skill for Life standard emphasises purposefulness.

> The ICT Functional Skills standards (QCA, 2007) state that *For ICT to be useful, learners must have the skills and confidence to apply, combine and adapt their ICT knowledge to new situations in their life and work.*

REFERENCES AND FURTHER READING REFERENCES AND FURTHER READING

Clarke, A, Reeve, A, Esson, J, Scott, J, Aldridge, F and Lindsay, K (2003) *Adult and Community Learning Laptop Initiative Evaluation.* London/Leicester: DfES NIACE.

Clarke, A (2006) 'Why ICT is a Skill for Life a personal view'. In *ICT Skills for Life Briefing: An independent professional update*, Issue 2, Febuary. Cambridge: Simon Boyd Publishing Ltd.

Clarke, A (2006) *Teaching Adults ICT Skills.* Exeter: Learning Matters.

Clarke, A (2007) *ICT Skill for Life.* London: Hodder Arnold.

Clarke, A (2008) *Digital Inclusion, Adults Learning.* Leicester: NIACE.

Communities and Local Government (2008) *Understanding Digital Exclusion: Research report* [online]. Available at: www.community.gov.uk [accessed 20 November 2008].

DfES (2003) *The Skills for Life Survey: A national needs and impact survey of literacy, numeracy and ICT.* London: Department for Education and Skills.

Digital Inclusion Panel (2004) *Enabling a Digitally United Kingdom.* London: Cabinet Office

Dutton, WH and Helsper, EJ (2007) *The Internet in Britain.* Oxford Internet Institute. Oxford: University of Oxford

Gartner (2004) *IT Insights: Trends and UK Skills Implications.* London/Stamford CT: Gartner Consulting.

Ipsos Mori (2008) *Digital Inclusion, social impact: a research study.* Sheffield: UK Online Centres.

JISC (2007) *In their own words: Exploring the learner's perspective on e-learning* [online]. Available at: www.jisc.ac.uk [accessed 2 April 2009].

Luger, E (2007) *ICT Skill for Life Investigation.* unpublished report for the DfES by NIACE.

NIACE (2005) *ICT Skill for Life – Action Research Project.* Draft Report to DfES [Accessed 2 April 2009] www.niace.org.uk/.

Prime Minister's Strategy Unit (2005) *Connecting the UK: the Digital Strategy* [online]. Available at: www.strategy.gov.uk [accessed November, 2008].

QCA (2007) *Functional Skills Standards: ICT* [online]. Available at: www.qca.org.uk/qca_6066.aspx [accessed December 2008].

Sabates, R (2007) *Use of ICT by young people in England.* Leicester: NIACE.

Selwyn, N (2002), 'Rethinking the Digital Divide in Adult Education: Neil Selwyn on a high profile adult education issue', *Adults Learning,* 13(10): *24.*

3
Importance of ICT in enabling users to participate in public life, society and the modern economy

This chapter will help you to:

- understand the importance of ICT in enabling users to participate in and gain access to society;
- understand the importance of ICT in enabling users to participate in and gain access to the modern economy.

Links to minimum core ICT

A1   Understand the importance of ICT in enabling users to participate in and gain
       access to society and the modern economy.
       The impact of limited ICT skills and access on a learner and their family.
       The impact of limited ICT skills on access to public services, rights and benefits,
       civil rights and community life.
       The impact of limited ICT skills and qualifications on obtaining and retaining employment.
       The increasing ICT skills demands of work processes and the service economy.

Links to LLUK Professional Standards

CP3.5 Make appropriate use of, and promote the benefits of new and emerging technologies.

Links to Diploma in Teaching in the Lifelong Learning Sector (DTLLS)

Unit 3 Enabling learning and assessment – how to apply minimum core specification in own
       specialist area.
Unit 4 Theories and principles for planning and enabling learning – how to apply minimum core
       specification in own specialist area.

Introduction

ICT continues to change the way that people live, work and learn. It is now normal to hear radio and television programmes read e-mails and text messages from viewers and listeners received during the programmes. You can book hotel rooms on the other side of the world or plan an independent journey across a continent. People can maintain relationships with complex networks of friends, families and colleagues through social networking, while almost every organisation, large and small, has a website. The majority of jobs now require some degree of ICT skills and it has been estimated that there is a 3 to 10 per cent income premium for work involving the use of technology (HM Government, 2008). Many companies now advertise vacancies on their websites and encourage online applications. FE colleges spent £250 million on ICT in 2005 with the blending of e-learning and traditional teaching methods now spread across the whole sector (BECTa, 2005).

ICT and society

The government's action plan, *Delivering Digital Inclusion* (HM Goverment, 2008), states that there are 17 million people who do not use computers or the internet. There is a strong correlation between digital and social exclusion with about six million people in both groups. This indicates that factors which socially exclude individuals also tend to make them digitally excluded. Factors that can contribute to social exclusion are:

- income;
- age;
- gender;
- location;
- ethnic origin;
- disability;
- learning difficulties.

Digital inclusion is not simply a matter of access to technology. It involves various factors such as personal relevance, ICT skills and understanding and meaningful access. Do people recognise the personal benefits of using technology? Do they have the skills required to use technology effectively and can they gain access to it? It is very different trying to use technology in a public location to the freedom of exploring the possibilities in your own home.

REFLECTIVE TASK

Digital exclusion

Reflect on your own use of technology and consider the implications if you did not have ICT skills and access to the internet. How would it influence your life?

There is a close link between age and internet access at home. Only 37 per cent of people over 65 years old have internet access at home compared to 67 per cent of all age groups. This reduces to 22 per cent for people over 75 years old. Nevertheless, older people who do use the internet tend to spend longer online than other users. This indicates the potential usefulness of the internet to older users (HM Government, 2008). Women over 65 years old spend less time on the internet than men of the same age. Almost half of the lowest socio-economic group (DE) do not have access to the internet at home or elsewhere. This demonstrates the link between poverty and digital exclusion.

Households without the internet

Many children live in households without access to ICT and the internet. While it has been demonstrated that home access can improve achievement, motivation and parental engagement (BECTa, 2008), there are over one million children without a computer at home This illustrates the impact on the children of families without access and the skills to use ICT. It is not enough that these children have the use of computers in school. They are disadvantaged compared to their peers when they go home. There is a correlation between households without access to ICT and the internet and social exclusion, so children from these families are likely to be disadvantaged in many ways such as low pay, educationally poor achievement and frequent unemployment.

For adult members of households without access to ICT and the internet there is a probability that finding and holding employment is likely to be more difficult due to the high proportion of jobs that require some degree of ICT skills. Equally, they will have slower and poorer access to information making them less informed about the world. This will include such areas as benefits, tax, government policy, local authority services and job opportunities.

Disabled users are one of the groups for whom most people can immediately see the benefits of ICT and access to the internet. However, only 36 per cent of disabled people in 2007 had access to the internet compared to 77 per cent of the whole population (Dutton and Helsper, 2007). ICT can assist disabled people overcome the barriers that they face to access information, services, education and employment. It can also allow them to write letters using speech synthesis or other adapted interface devices, participate with people through social networking, maintain family relationships with communication technology and shop for daily needs without the need to leave their homes. Without ICT and the internet, disabled people may well be isolated in their own homes, unable to function independently and reliant on family and friends for basic necessities.

Citizenship

There has been a progressive effort to make information and services available online. This has resulted in more information being available about government than at any other time in our history. However, it is only available if you have access to ICT equipment and the skills to use it effectively.

Every local authority provides extensive information about its budgets, services and activities on its website while the e-mail addresses of Members of Parliament are available on the House of Commons website. Many members also have personal websites and blogs explaining their views and ideas. They are keen for their constituents to communicate with them through e-mail. Many everyday services are now provided online such as road tax and income tax self-assessment. HM Revenue and Customs have mounted an extensive campaign on posters and through television advertising to encourage people to submit their assessment online.

The alternative to accessing services and information online is travelling to or telephoning a public office and asking for information, obtaining paper forms or seeking interviews with staff. At the least it is time consuming, inconvenient and assumes you know what to ask for. Online information presents the services and information to you. The physical alternative is that a leaflet is displayed in a public office or in the library or citizens' advice bureau. For people with family commitments, care responsibilities, limited time or who simply live in remote locations, it is significantly more challenging to keep up to date if they cannot gain access to online services through ICT.

SCENARIO STUDY – ROAD TAX

In order to tax your car online you need a copy of the reminder (V11). You access the Driver and Vehicle Licensing Agency (DVLA) website and follow the online instructions which involve entering the code on the V11 form. The system checks that your vehicle is insured and has a valid MOT. It takes a few minutes.

In contrast, to tax your car in person involves a trip to a Post Office. You need to complete the V11 form and take copies of your insurance certificate or cover note and a valid MOT certificate. This takes far longer than a few minutes.

Discussion

This may seem a trivial example but if the individuals renewing the road tax are disabled, are carers, live in a rural area or are simply busy with family and work responsibilities they are at a significant disadvantage. If you add all the other losses in convenience that a lack of online access brings, then it is a major disadvantage.

Directgov (http://www.direct.gov.uk/en/index.htm) is the government's website for citizens. It offers on its home page links to information about:

- education and learning;
- motoring;
- home and community;
- employment;
- money, tax and benefits;
- health and well-being;
- travel and transport;
- environment and greener living;
- crime, justice and the law;
- government, citizens and rights.

This indicates the scale of online information available that is accessible in a few moments in your own home. The alternatives are far more difficult, if not impossible. A large library would probably not be able to offer you this range. The information is practical help with living in a modern society. Without it, you may well miss out on benefits, not be aware of your rights (e.g. redundancy), be unable to contribute fully to your community and simply waste a lot of effort to achieve a poorer result.

PRACTICAL TASK PRACTICAL TASK PRACTICAL TASK PRACTICAL TASK PRACTICAL TASK

Seeking information

If you had to find out what benefits you were entitled to and how to claim them should you be made redundant tomorrow, how would you find out if you could not use the internet to search for information?

ICT and modern economy

ICT skills are now reqiured in 77 per cent of all jobs, with a third of all employees regarding the internet as essential (e-skills, 2008). The type of use varies considerably between different occupations with the overwhelming majority of managers and administrators using technology. These proportions are rapidly increasing, so within a few years it is likely that all jobs will require staff with ICT skills in some form or another. E-skills (2008) reported that older workers (i.e. over 55 years old) have seen the quickest growth in using ICT at work of any group since 2001. In 2008, 72 per cent of older employees use ICT.

The demand for employees with higher levels of ICT skills has been growing over several years, with the demand in 2008 focused on levels 2, 3 and higher (e-skills, 2008). E-skills (2008) estimate, that current demand for existing employees to up skill to level 2, 3 and above being respectively, 31 per cent, 48 per cent and 15 per cent. The demand in 2010, they estimate will continue to focus on higher levels but with the levels being respectively, 19 per cent, 41 per cent and 28 per cent. This indicates that as technology develops, employers will want a workforce with the skills to exploit it effectively. For unemployed people seeking employment it is clear that at least level 1 skills are required, with the ability to progress to level 3 and above in the future.

REFLECTIVE TASK
REFLECTIVE TASK

REFLECTIVE TASK

Consider the ICT skills required for an occupation you know. How have they changed over recent years?

The government has identified English, Mathematics and ICT as functional skills. They are the practical skills that allow individuals to work confidently, effectively and independently in life (QCA, 2008). In 2004 e-skills, the ICT sector skills council estimated that nine out of ten new jobs required ICT skills. They concluded that without the required skills, individuals would lose out on employment opportunities. Without ICT skills it will be increasingly difficult to obtain employment except in unskilled low paid jobs. This is compounded by the trend among employers to want employees to continue to develop even higher levels of ICT skills. It is likely that unless individuals' ICT skills improve, they will find it more difficult to retain employment.

SCENARIO STUDY – FARMERS

It is perhaps not obvious why hill farmers would need to be able to use ICT as part of their business and lives. However, there are many critical factors that make it vital for a farmer to be able to use ICT. They include:

1. Many forms and returns that farmers need to make to obtain payments under the common agricultural policy are provided online.
2. A farm is a business in which records need to be kept so that costs and incomes can be monitored and regulations (e.g. animal movement certification) followed. Communication channels to customers and suppliers are required.
3. Farms are often in isolated rural areas and the nature of farm life makes it difficult to leave the farm to access services which can be obtained online.
4. Many small farmers are seeking to diversify into other areas such as tourism, farm shops, breeding sheep dogs and selling ice cream. A website is an excellent means of advertising new services.

There are probably many more reasons but technology is vital to survive and prosper in a modern society.

Dutton and Helsper (2007) showed that people who have access to the internet are more likely to have access to other forms of ICT. In their report they state that internet users are more likely to have a digital camera, mp3 player, webcam and PDA than non-users. In 2007, 32 per cent of people in Britain had never used a computer.

Technology provides the opportunity to continue to learn away from the face-to-face classroom setting. Groups of learners can continue to communicate through e-mails so that mutual support and group activities can continue. Learners can access resources on the internet, whether these are college material that can be downloaded from its virtual learning environment or other content on independent websites. Of course, this is not possible unless learners have both access to the technology and the skills to use it.

Learners who have access to technology in their own homes can choose when, where and how to participate in learning activities. This is vital for learners with busy lives or family and work responsibilities. It allows them to organise their learning at the most convenient and suitable times. There is a lot of community-based access to technology but inevitably it needs to be booked or is limited either in the time it is available or in sophistication. At the least, community technology will not provide learners with the freedom of when, where and how they learn.

Community provision is available through:

- UK Online centres – there are several thousand centres located in the most deprived wards in the country. These often provide more than access with support available and training in the use of ICT and the internet.
- Public libraries – free access (or with a small charge) is widely available but support may be limited and often there are time limits imposed on using the technology. Training courses are sometimes provided through adult education providers in libraries.
- Many organisations are providing access to the internet through wireless connections. These are not always free to use and the learner will need a wireless-enabled computer to use them.

PRACTICAL TASK PRACTICAL TASK PRACTICAL TASK PRACTICAL TASK PRACTICAL TASK

Community access

Use a community- or library-based computer to access the college website and download some materials. How easy was it to undertake this task? How would learners dependent on community access be able to participate in online learning activities?

Access the internet through a public wireless connection to gain experience of it strengths and weaknesses.

Education

Following NIACE's surveys into participation over 20 years, Sargant and Aldridge (2002) considered the persistent pattern that emerges of adult participation in learning. It showed that socio-economic class remains the dominant factor in participation. Sixty per cent of upper and middle class respondents (AB) were learning, compared to 25 per cent of semi skilled, unskilled and people on the lowest levels of income (DE). *Delivering Digital Inclusion* (HM Goverment, 2008) showed the correlation between social disadvantage and digital exclusion so that considering these factors together it is likely that people on the lowest incomes were both unlikely to participate in learning and also not have access to technology

The key difference between an adult learner and a school child is that the adult chooses to take part in the course. However, adults with a poor experience of compulsory education will be reluctant to return to learning once they have left school. This is often apparent in disadvantaged adults who are unwilling to take part in what they regard as formal or institutional learning while often being content to participate in community-based provision. This may be because they do not identify community provision with their previous experience. The motivational effects of learning about and through ICT on learners with literacy and numeracy needs may also be due to learners not linking it to previous poor experiences but rather identifying it as different and interesting.

The trend towards the application of e-learning across FE and skills assumes that learners will be able to participate in technology-enhanced programmes. However, since adults who lack ICT are more likely to be socially disadvantaged, they are already less likely to participate in education. The effect may be to decrease participation and retention.

ICT skills development

E-skills and Gartner reported in 2004 that, of the 20 million employed users of ICT, 40 per cent had received no training, illustrating that many people had independently developed their skills. This is supported by the outcomes of the National Office of Statistics survey of internet use (2007) and the Oxford internet Survey (Dutton and Helsper, 2007) findings which showed a culture of self-help in relation to technology. There are also many voluntary and community organisations, such as the network of UK Online centres, that offer informal support to develop ICT skills.

The ability to learn independently is an important skill but may result in only partial coverage of the range of skills required to be computer literate. However, formal courses also have weaknesses in that they are often focused on developing the skills of using a range of the more popular applications with relatively little effort in relation to transferable skills or dealing with the dynamic nature of ICT.

It is difficult to make assumptions about the level of an individual's ICT skills simply based on their educational record. They may well have high-level, self-taught skills or great skills in using applications but little understanding of transfer or coping with change. This would suggest the need to assess the learners' skills in your context.

REFLECTIVE TASK

Self help

Consider your own experience of independently learning ICT skills. How effective and efficient was your own effort?

Spiky profiles

It is now widely accepted that learners have spiky ICT skills profiles. This may be either a result of independent learning that is likely to relate to access to particular technologies or simply focused ICT education and training courses. It also reflects on the individual's ICT needs when skills have been developed as a result of a need to be able to use technology for a particular purpose.

The spiky profile may result in a person who is an expert user of a digital camera, able to edit photographs with considerable skill and upload them on to a website but unable to use a spreadsheet. Alternatively, a user with considerable ability to use Office applications may have no experience of using a PDA or undertaking advanced searches of the internet. Spiky profiles are not necessarily negative, since they will often have been developed to meet the learners' needs in their employment or social life. It does mean that you cannot assume, however, high-level skills in one area are going to be matched in others.

The ITQ qualification is based around the concept of spiky profiles whereby employers are encouraged to identify the profile of skills required for a particular job and to train their staff to meet the profile. The outcomes are employees with spiky profiles but ones that match their employers' needs.

REFLECTIVE TASK

Your own profile

Consider your own profile – how was it developed? What were the main influences on the skills profile you have developed?

Literacy

ICT has its own language and jargon. There are many technical terms that learners need to understand. This may result in courses that demand a high level of literacy skills from a learner. Many people in the country have problems with literacy. It is therefore possible to disadvantage learners through presenting a course with too many literacy demands. This may be in the form of learning materials that are not easy to read or which use advanced vocabulary.

PRACTICAL TASK PRACTICAL TASK PRACTICAL TASK PRACTICAL TASK PRACTICAL TASK

Readability

Assess the readability of your learning materials for a course that you teach. Microsoft Word provides a readability score (Tools Menu, Options and Spelling and Grammar tab) – the readability statistics are shown after you have spell checked your work.

A SUMMARY OF KEY POINTS

> ICT continues to change the way that people live, work and learn.

> *Delivering Digital Inclusion* (HM Government, 2008) states that there are 17 million people who do not use computers or the internet. There is a strong correlation between digital and social exclusion with about six million people in both groups.

> Digital inclusion involves many factors such as personal relevance, ICT skills and understanding and meaningful access to technology.

> Only 37 per cent of people over 65 years old have internet access at home compared to 67 per cent of all age groups. However, older people who do use the internet tend to spend longer online than other users.

> Almost half of the lowest socio-economic group (DE) do not have access to the internet at home or elsewhere.

> There are over one million children without a computer at home while it has been demonstrated that home access can improve achievement, motivation and parental engagement (BECTa, 2008).

> Only 36 per cent of disabled people in 2007 had access to the internet compared to 77 per cent of the whole population (Dutton and Helsper, 2007).

> More information is now available about government than at any other time in our history.

> Directgov (http://www.direct.gov.uk/en/index.htm) is the government's website for citizens.

> ICT skills are now required in 77 per cent of all jobs, with a third of all employees now regarding the internet as essential (e-skills, 2008).

> The type of ICT use varies considerably between different occupations.

> E-skills (2008) reported that older workers (i.e. over 55 years old) have seen the quickest growth in using ICT at work of any group since 2001. In 2008, 72 per cent of older employees used ICT.

> E-skills (2008) estimate that current demand for existing employees to up skill would continue to grow.

> The government has identified English, Mathematics and ICT as functional skills.

> Dutton and Helsper (2007) showed that people who have access to the internet are more likely to have access to other forms of ICT.

> Learners who have access to technology in their own homes can choose when, where and how to participate in online learning activities.

> Community provision is available through UK Online centres, public libraries and access to the internet through wireless connections.

> It is likely that people on the lowest incomes are both less likely to participate in learning and have access to technology

> The motivational effects of learning about and through ICT on learners with literacy and numeracy needs may also be due to their not linking it to previous poor experiences but rather identifying it as different and interesting.

> Many people have independently developed their ICT skills. It is therefore difficult to make assumptions about the level of an individual's ICT skills based simply on their educational record.

> It is now widely accepted that learners have spiky ICT skills profiles, whereby they may be expert users of some technologies and beginners in other areas.

> ICT has its own language and jargon. There are many technical terms that learners are required to understand. This may result in courses that demand a high level of literacy skills from a learner.

REFERENCES AND FURTHER READING REFERENCES AND FURTHER READING

BECTa (2005), *ICT and e-learning in Further Education.* Coventry: BECTa ICT Research.

BECTa (2008), *Home Access* [online]. Available at: www.becta.org.uk/ [accessed December 2008].

Dutton, W.H and Helsper, E.J (2007) *The internet in Britain.* Oxford internet Institute. Oxford: University of Oxford

e-skills and Gartner (2004) *IT Insights: Trends and UK Skills Implications.* London: E-skills UK, Sector Skills Council, Gartner Consulting.

e-skills (2008) *Technology Counts, IT & Telecoms Insights 2008.* London: E-skills UK, Sector Skills Council

HM Government (2008) *Delivering Digital Inclusion: An Action Plan for Consultation, Communities and Local Government.* London: HM Government.

QCA (2008), *Functional Skills* [online]. Available at: www.qca.org.uk/qca_6062.aspx [accessed December 2008].

Sargant, N and Aldridge, F (2002) *Adult Learning and social division; a persistent pattern, Volume 1.* Leicester: NIACE.

Sargant, N and Aldridge, F (2002) *Adult Learning and social division; a persistent pattern, Volume 2.* Leicester: NIACE.

4
Main learning disabilities and difficulties relating to ICT learning and skills development

This chapter will help you to:

- be aware of the impact that learning difficulties and disabilities, as described in *Delivering Skills for Life: Introducing Access for All* (DfES, nd), can have on ICT learning;
- be aware of the resources, specialist equipment, teaching strategies and referral procedures which can help learners overcome their difficulties in ICT use and learning.

Links to minimum core ICT

A1   Awareness of the impact that learning difficulties and disabilities, as described in *Delivering Skills for Life: Introducing Access for All*, can have on ICT learning. Supportive strategies that learners can use to overcome difficulties in their ICT use and learning.
Awareness of the resources, specialist equipment, teaching strategies and referral rocedures which can help learners overcome their difficulties in ICT use and learning.

Links to LLUK Professional Standards

AK3.1 Issues of equality, diversity and inclusion.
AP3.1 Apply principles to evaluate and develop own practice in promoting equality and inclusive learning and engaging with diversity.
AK6.1 Relevant statutory requirements and codes of practice.
BP2.4 Apply flexible and varied delivery methods as appropriate to teaching and learning practice.
BK5.2 Ways to ensure that resources used are inclusive, promote equality and support delivery.
CK3.5 Ways to support learners in the use of new and emerging technologies in own specialist area.
CP3.5 Make appropriate use of, and promote the benefits of new and emerging technologies.
FP2.1 Provide effective learning support, within the boundaries of the teaching role.

Links to Certificate in Teaching in the Lifelong Learning Sector (CTLLS)

Unit 2 Planning and enabling learning.

Links to Diploma in Teaching in the Lifelong Learning Sector (DTLLS)

Unit 2 Planning and enabling learning.
Unit 3 Enabling learning and assessment.
Unit 4 Theories and principles for planning and enabling learning.

Introduction

Technology can provide considerable support to disabled learners and those with learning difficulties. Unfortunately, it can also be a barrier if used inappropriately. The Special Educational Needs and Disability Act 2001 (SENDA) (Office of Public Sector Information, nd) extended the Disability and Discrimination Act (DDA) into education. Disabled learners have the right to access learning in post-16 education. Providers must not act 'less favourably' towards disabled learners and must 'offer reasonable adjustments' which will ensure that disabled learners are not substantially disadvantaged in relation to those who are not disabled. The act applies to all staff and the legal liability applies if any single member of staff is aware of the individual's disability.

Disabilities are not always obvious and individuals need to feel confident and comfortable when talking to you about their needs. In some cases learners may not be aware of their disability (e.g. dyslexia) and you will need to call for specialist help and support. In some cases, learners may want their disability to remain confidential. The key step is to create an environment in which the learners trust you and are willing to discuss their needs with you.

The information that a learner provides is confidential and should not be disclosed to anyone else without their permission. It can, however, be very difficult to make reasonable adjustments on your own. You need to obtain the learner's consent to discuss their needs with other staff. They are more likely to consent if they can identify a positive attitude from you and your employer towards them.

SCENARIO STUDY – CREATING AN ENVIRONMENT

You are faced with a new group of learners and want to create an environment in which they will feel comfortable discussing their needs with you in private. The group do not know each other. They do not know you. They may have little knowledge of the provider or equally have doubts about them and the course. What do you do?

Discussion

There are various things that you might do but here are some ideas:

1. The initial issue is to break down any barriers and encourage the learners to talk. You could, for example, ask the learners to form small groups, introduce themselves and then ask their colleagues to introduce them to the whole class.
2. Explain how the college and you can help disabled learners and then provide opportunities for learners to speak to you in private.
3. Provide information on a handout so they can take it away and consider if they need support.
4. Find time to speak to each learner individually about their learning.
5. Regularly review their progress.

What else could you do?

Jacobsen (2000) helped to develop a charter for learning for people with learning difficulties. It was developed by asking individual learners from across Britain what they wanted. It provides a clear insight into their views:

- the right to speak up;
- the right to choose to go to classes;
- the right to have support;
- the right to have the chance to make friends;
- the right to have fun learning;
- the right to good access;
- the right not to be bullied;
- the right to be treated as an adult with respect;
- the right to have clear information that they can understand;
- the right to have good teaching;
- the right to do a course and get a job;
- the right to learn in a nice place.

Although the charter was developed prior to SENDA becoming law, it still provides a powerful insight into learners' expectations.

Learning difficulties and disabilities

Learning difficulties and disabilities will have a wide range of impacts on individuals. Some adults will have been successful learners while others may have had poor experiences of education. They may well have done well in some areas and less well in others so that they have a spiky profile of skills and knowledge. This may be presented as having outstanding abilities in certain activities while finding others extremely challenging. It has always been good practice to build on learners' strengths and this is equally true for individuals with learning difficulties and disabilities. Adult learners are experts about the effects of their disabilities on their learning, so discuss approaches with them. It is important not to stereotype learners but to treat them as individuals.

Delivering Skills for Life: Introducing Access for All (DfES, nd) provides many examples of the effects of learning difficulties and disabilities on learning. The list below gives some illustrations of the effects:

- Deaf and partially hearing learners may find it more difficult to develop language skills (e.g. spoken and written).
- Blind and partially sighted learners rely more on their hearing to obtain information than do other learners.
- Learners with mental ill health may suffer more stress than other learners during assessment.
- Dyslexic learners may have difficulties organising their work.
- Physically disabled learners may have accessibility problems with buildings, classrooms and computers.
- Individuals with learning difficulties may have spiky learning profiles.
- Learners with autistic spectrum disorders may find even small changes to routines unsettling.

PRACTICAL TASK PRACTICAL TASK PRACTICAL TASK PRACTICAL TASK PRACTICAL TASK

Effects

Obtain a copy of *Delivering Skills for Life: Introducing Access for All* (DfES), nd and consider the impact that learning difficulties such as dyslexia may have on an individual. In particular, consider how you could support them. You may want to access the AbilityNet and TechDis websites which both offer considerable support in relation to the use of technology.

Overcoming difficulties

Delivering Skills for Life: Introducing Access for All (DfES, nd) provides numerous examples of approaches to learning that may assist or support learners. Again, it is important to consider learners as individuals with their own strengths and weaknesses. Some examples of approaches that may be useful are:

- face deaf and partially hearing learners and speak clearly and naturally;
- ask other learners to introduce themselves before they speak so that blind and partially sighted learners can identify them;
- include a range of different activities in each classroom or session for learners with mental ill health;
- support dyslexic learners to identify how dyslexia is affecting their learning;
- consider the access to the classroom for physically disabled learners in advance of the start of the programme;
- encourage learners with learning difficulties to take responsibility for their own learning;
- create routines for learners with autistic spectrum disorders.

PRACTICAL TASK PRACTICAL TASK PRACTICAL TASK PRACTICAL TASK PRACTICAL TASK

Approaches

Obtain a copy of *Delivering Skills for Life: Introducing Access for All* (DfES, nd) and consider the range of approaches for disabled learners such as deaf or partially hearing people.

Delivering Skills for Life: Introducing Access for All (DfES, nd) provides a set of principles for curriculum delivery. They can be summarised as:

- assess the learners and use their skills and knowledge as a foundation on which to take them forward;
- have discussions with the learners to identify what helps and hinders their learning;
- employ the learners' context and language as far as you can;
- find out what motivates them and use it to help them develop;
- aim high and help the learners to succeed;
- use their learning styles to guide your approach and help the learners understand their learning preferences;
- ensure that the learning environment and materials are suitable for the individual;
- use alternative methods if learners are not succeeding;
- match activity, skills and individual needs to make sure they are suitable;
- check the learners' understanding regularly;
- regularly review progress with the learner;
- build on the learners' strengths;
- learners will often have a spiky profile of skills and knowledge.

Technology

Technology provides a range of tools that can assist and support disabled learners and those with learning difficulties. Some examples of the use of technology (DfES, nd) are:

- video conferencing can assist deaf and partially hearing learners to communicate over long distances;
- computers can present information as speech for blind and partially sighted learners;
- word processors can support dyslexic learners' spelling and presentation of work;
- assistive technology can help physically disabled learners to access the internet and use computers in their learning;
- technology can often provide a motivating learning environment for learners with learning difficulties.

There is a vast range of possible applications for the use of technology. Microsoft Windows operating system and Internet Explorer browser both come equipped with functions to assist disabled users.

Microsoft Windows

Microsoft Windows provides several functions to help and support disabled users, offering the means to customise the system. The functions are available in the Control Panel of the system (Start menu, Control Panel and Ease of Access Center – Microsoft Windows Vista). Figure 4.1 shows the Ease of Access Center display. Alternatively you can access the functions by using the All programs menu, Accessories and Ease of Access. The functions are designed to help blind and partially sighted, deaf and partially hearing and physically disabled users. They provide considerable control over the display of information and therefore can also assist other users (e.g. dyslexic users and people with learning difficulties).

Figure 4.1 Ease of Access Center

Designed to help partially sighted users, the Magnifier is a moveable on-screen magnifying glass that you can also adjust to provide different degrees of magnification. In addition, there is a range of other functions to help make the display easier to see. Figure 4.2 illustrates the options shown when the Make the computer easier to see link is selected. The options are:

- High Contrast – this maximises the contrast between text and background, making it easy to read;
- Narrator – this option reads aloud any text that is displayed. The computer does need speakers or headphones;
- Magnifier.

REFLECTIVE TASK

Magnifier

Use the options to access the magnifier function and carry out a task using the system such as writing a letter or sending an e-mail. Reflect on the experience, comparing undertaking the task with and without the magnifier.

You can also adjust the screen resolution and the size of the text displayed by using other options available through the Control Panel. The Personalisation icon provides access to functions with which you can:

- change the colours and appearance of windows;
- alter the background display;
- change sounds;
- select a different mouse pointer;
- change the resolution;
- adjust the font sizes.

These functions enable you to customise the display to meet the needs of the learner.

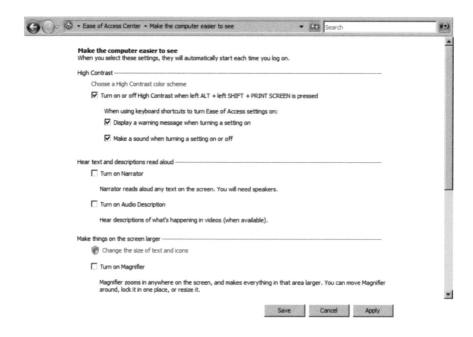

Figure 4.2 Make the computer easier to see

Physically disabled learners may find the keyboard difficult to use, so Microsoft Windows provides an on-screen keyboard that you use with a pointing device such as a mouse. Figure 4.3 shows the on-screen keyboard. The Ease of Access Center also provides options (i.e. Make the Keyboard easier to use) to help make the keyboard Easier to Use. These include:

- controlling the mouse using the keyboard arrow keys;
- sticky keys that allow you to use keyboard shortcuts by pressing one key at a time;
- toggle keys – you hear a sound when you press the Caps lock, Num lock or Scroll lock.

PRACTICAL TASK PRACTICAL TASK PRACTICAL TASK PRACTICAL TASK PRACTICAL TASK

On-screen keyboard

Use the options to access the on-screen keyboard and carry out a task using the system, such as writing a letter or sending an e-mail. Reflect on the experience, comparing undertaking the task with and without the on-screen keyboard.

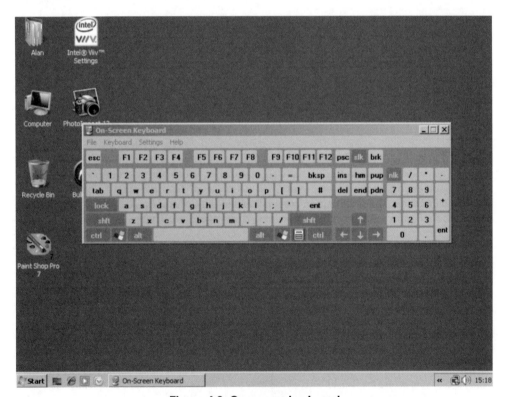

Figure 4.3 On-screen keyboard

Microsoft Windows (Ease of Access) also provides functions to help people use the mouse. Figure 4.4 shows the main options. You can change the appearance of the mouse pointer to make it more visible and control of the mouse can be switched to the keyboard arrow keys. More functions are available by clicking on the Mouse Setting link which opens a window providing options to make the mouse buttons suitable for a left-handed user, to control the speed of double clicking and to make dragging easier. These options are also available in the Control Panel by clicking on the mouse icon.

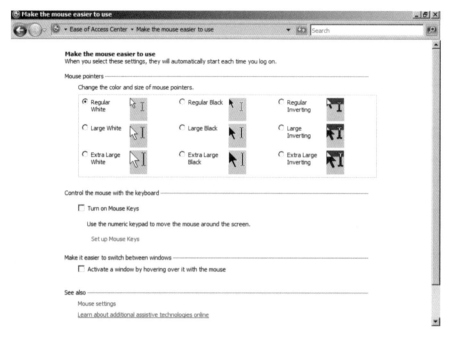

Figure 4.4 Make the mouse easier to use

Figure 4.1 shows an option called Narrator that reads aloud any text that appears on the screen. This is useful to blind or partially sighted users. Windows also supports voice control. Speech recognition is very useful for a range of disabled users and those with learning difficulties. These functions are available in the Control Panel Speech Recognition options icon. Figure 4.5 shows the different options available. These include:

- voice control;
- train the computer to recognise your voice;
- tutorial;
- set up a microphone.

PRACTICAL TASK PRACTICAL TASK PRACTICAL TASK PRACTICAL TASK PRACTICAL TASK

Narrator

Use the options to access the Narrator function and carry out a task using the system, such as writing a letter or sending an e-mail. Reflect on the experience, comparing undertaking the task with and without the narrator.

Browsers

A key part of ICT is communication technology and using the internet to locate and use information. Browsers (e.g. Internet Explorer) provide the window through which you observe the world wide web. The ability of a browser to be customised to meet individual needs is therefore crucial.

Internet Explorer is still the most widely used browser but other products also exist such as Opera, Firefox, Netspace and Google Chrome. Additionally, there are also products such as Jaws, which is a screen reader that works with some browsers whereby website content is read aloud to users. Jaws will also read e-mail messages.

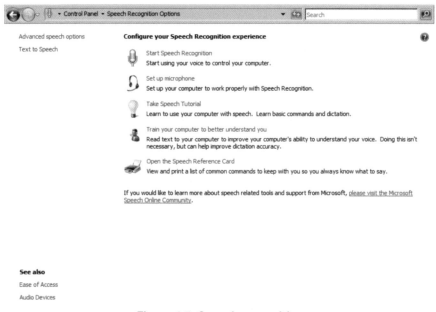

Figure 4.5 Speech recognition

This section is based on Internet Explorer 7, a browser that allows you to:

- adjust the size of displayed text;
- magnify the display;
- change the colours;
- control presentation of information through your own style sheet.

To adjust the size of text in Internet Explorer you need to select the Page menu then highlight Text Size option to reveal five sizes of text to choose from. They are:

- largest;
- large;
- medium;
- small;
- smallest.

In addition to changing the text size, you can magnify the information using the zoom option which is available in the Page menu and then highlighting the Zoom option. This reveals a series of zoom percentages from 50 per cent to 400 per cent. You can also control the zoom in and out through keyboard using Ctrl + to zoom in and Ctrl – to zoom out.

PRACTICAL TASK PRACTICAL TASK PRACTICAL TASK PRACTICAL TASK PRACTICAL TASK

Text size

Use the browser options to explore the different text sizes and access a range of websites, considering the effects of the changes.

Controlling the colours used is important in assisting the readability and understanding of the information displayed. Microsoft Windows Vista allows you to control the displayed colours through the Internet Options, which are accessed through the Control Panel. When you select the Internet Options icon, a window opens (shown on the left of the display). You need to click on the Accessibility button to open a new window (on the right of the display) and select Ignore colors specified on webpages. This is actioned when you select the OK button. The effect of this change is that colours shown on webpages are the ones you have selected for your computer.

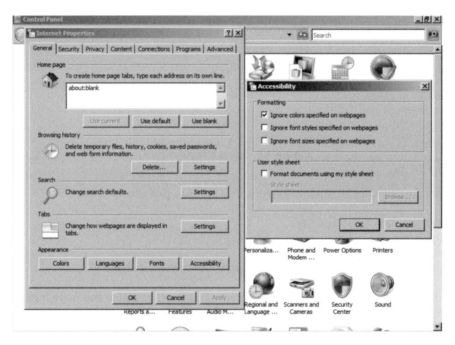

Figure 4.6 Controlling colours

To change the colours that Microsoft Windows is using, click on the Colors button in the internet Options window. This will open a window called Colors along with a button called Use windows colors checked with a tick. If you untick the option by clicking on it, the four types of colours below (i.e. text, background, visited and unvisted) can be changed. They are changed by clicking on the colours shown to open a palette for you to choose from.

PRACTICAL TASK PRACTICAL TASK PRACTICAL TASK PRACTICAL TASK PRACTICAL TASK

Change colours

Use the Microsoft Windows options to change the colours in windows and to control the display of colours on websites. Compare the effects of the changes by visiting websites before and after the changes.

In addition to controlling the use of colour by making websites use the colours that you have chosen for Microsoft Windows, you can also use style sheets (i.e. a template) to control the fonts and colour displayed. You need first of all to create a style sheet. The W3C consortium offers some standard style sheets. These are available from www.w3.org/StyleSheets/Core/. W3C is the consortium that has established standards for website accessibility. In order to use style sheets, you must access Internet Options and select the Accessibility button to reveal the Accessibility window (figure 4.6), then choose Format documents using my style sheet.

Assistive technologies

There is a wide range of assistive technologies available to help disabled learners and those with learning difficulties. They take various forms such as:

- alternative pointing devices, rather than using a mouse;
- different types of keyboards;
- speech control applications.

There are many to choose from and it is important to take expert advice about the ones that are most appropriate. Learners may well have experience of what they need, so an obvious starting place is to ask them what they normally use and what is effective. Your employer is likely to have access to specialist advice so it is important to be aware of how you refer learners.

There are two organisations that offer support for disabled learners and those with learning difficulties. They are:

- AbilityNet;
- TechDis.

AbilityNet is a charity that aims to help disabled people use ICT and access the internet while TechDis is an organisation that aims to help learners by improving accessibility. TechDis offers a range of publications for people working in education.

PRACTICAL TASK PRACTICAL TASK PRACTICAL TASK PRACTICAL TASK PRACTICAL TASK

Support

Visit the AbilityNet and TechDis websites and explore what help they can provide for you and your learners.

A SUMMARY OF KEY POINTS

> The SENDA 2001 extended the DDA Act into education. Disabled learners have the right to access learning in Post-16 education. Providers must not act towards disabled learners 'less favourably' and must 'offer reasonable adjustments'.

> Reasonable adjustments are required to ensure that disabled learners are not substantially disadvantaged in relation to learners who are not disabled.

> Disabilities are not always obvious. Individuals need to feel confident and comfortable that they can talk to you about their needs.

> The information that a learner provides you with is confidential and should not be disclosed to anyone else without their permission.

> Learning difficulties and disabilities will have a very wide range of impacts on individuals. It is important not to stereotype learners or make assumptions. You need to treat each person as an individual.

> *Delivering Skills for Life: Introducing Access for All* (DfES, nd) provides many examples of the effects of learning difficulties and disabilities on learning.

> *Delivering Skills for Life: Introducing Access for All* (DfES, nd) provides many examples of approaches to learning that may assist or support learners.

> *Delivering Skills for Life: Introducing Access for All* (DfES, nd) provides a set of principles for curriculum delivery.

> Microsoft Windows provides several functions to help and support disabled users. The functions are available in the Control Panel of the system (Start menu, Control Panel and Ease of Access Center – Microsoft Windows Vista).

> The Magnifier is a moveable on-screen magnifying glass that you can adjust to provide different degrees of magnification.

> High contrast – this maximises the contrast between text and background to make it easy to read.

> Narrator – this option reads aloud any text that is displayed. The computer does need speakers or headphones.

> The Personalisation icon provides access to functions through which you can change the colours, appearance, sound, background, mouse pointers, resolution and font sizes.

> Microsoft Windows provides an on-screen keyboard that you use with a pointing device such as a mouse.

> The operation of the mouse can be adjusted in Microsoft Windows (e.g. using the keyboard arrow keys).

> Microsoft Windows supports voice control through the Control Panel Speech Recognition options icon.

> Internet Explorer is still the most widely used browser but other products are also widely used such as Opera, Firefox, Netspace and Google Chrome. There are also products such as Jaws which is a screen reader that works with some browsers to read aloud website content.

> Internet Explorer 7 and Microsoft Windows allows you to adjust the size of displayed text, magnify the display, change colours and control presentation of information through your own style sheet.

> There are a wide range of assistive technologies available to assist disabled learners and learners with learning difficulties.

> It is important to take expert advice about which assistive technologies are most appropriate.

> It is important to be aware of how you refer learners for help with assistive technologies.

> Two organisations offer support for disabled learners and those with learning difficulties. They are AbilityNet and TechDis.

REFERENCES AND FURTHER READING REFERENCES AND FURTHER READING

AbilityNet (nd) *Advice and resources about accessibility* [online]. Available at:
www.abilitynet.org.uk/ [accessed 16 January 2009].

BBC (nd) *Accessibility* [online]. Available at: www.bbc.co.uk/accessibility/ [accessed 18 January
2009].

BECTa, *Advice about accessibility* [online]. Available at: about.becta.org.uk/ [accessed 18 January
2009].

DfES (nd) *Delivering Skills for Life: Introducing Access for All*, London: DfES.

Jacobsen, Y (2000) *Charter for Learning* [online]. Available at:
http://archive.niace.org.uk/Research/HDE/Projects/charter/minicharter.htm [accessed 16
January 2009].

JISC (nd) *Resources for staff* [online]. Available at: www.TechDis.ac.uk/ [accessed 16
January 2009].

Office of Public Sector Information (nd) *SENDA* [online]. Available at:
www.opsi.gov.uk/ACTS/acts2001/ukpga_20010010_en_1 [accessed 16 January 2009].

Royal National Institute for the Blind (RNIB) (nd) [online]. Available at:
www.rnib.org.uk/xpedio/groups/public/documents/Code/public_rnib008789.hcsp [accessed

TechDis (nd) *Advice and resources about accessibility* [online]. Available at: www.techdis.ac.uk/
[accessed 18 January 2009].

5
Potential barriers that inhibit ICT skills development

This chapter will help you to:

- be aware of personal factors that may inhibit the development of ICT skills;
- be aware of the institutional factors that may inhibit the development of ICT skills;
- be aware of the teaching and learning factors that may inhibit the development of ICT skills.

Links to minimum core ICT

A1   Awareness of the personal, institutional and teaching and learning factors that may inhibit the development of ICT skills.

Links to LLUK Professional Standards

AK4.2   The impact of own practice on individuals and their learning.

BP2.4   Apply flexible and varied delivery methods as appropriate to teaching and learning practice.

BP5.1   Select and develop a range of effective resources, including appropriate use of new and emerging technologies.

CK3.5   Ways to support learners in the use of new and emerging technologies in own specialist area.

CP3.5   Make appropriate use of, and promote the benefits of new and emerging technologies.

EP1.1   Use appropriate forms of assessment and evaluate their effectiveness in producing information useful to the teacher and the learner.

Links to Certificate in Teaching in the Lifelong Learning Sector (CTLLS)

Unit 2 Planning and enabling learning.

Links to Diploma in Teaching in the Lifelong Learning Sector (DTLLS)

Unit 2 Planning and enabling learning.
Unit 3 Enabling learning and assessment.
Unit 4 Theories and principles for planning and enabling learning.

Introduction

People's motivation towards ICT will have a large impact on their willingness to develop the necessary skills and understanding. Dutton and Helsper (2007) reported on the attitudes towards the internet of non-users and users. They found that non-users tended to believe that the internet was complex and frustrating to use, while a large minority (40 per cent) did not believe that it was going to improve their lives. These factors would have a substantial effect on the learners' willingness to start to develop skills and also on their belief that they were able to do so. Any training or education programme would need to overcome these views so that learners could gain confidence to make progress. On a more positive note, 76 per cent of internet non-users felt that it was an efficient way of accessing information. This might provide a useful starting point for developing skills.

Ofcom's Consumer Panel (2006) undertook a survey to investigate older people's attitudes to the internet. A key finding was that non-users of communication technologies had not rejected them. A majority of non-users would be interested in learning about communication technologies if the conditions were right for them. Those classified as 'Self Starters' learning to use communication technology often gave reasons linked to family needs, such as communicating with children based overseas.

The obstacles to using the internet raised by non-users were diverse but included issues such as:

- lack of experience with computers linked to limited confidence that they could learn the required skills;
- computing appeared complex and used an unfamiliar language;
- people found it difficult to see how the internet would be useful to them;
- some non-users had had poor experiences on computer courses;
- some were reluctant to use computers for fear that they would fail;
- financial worries;
- limited time to learn;
- concerns about privacy and security of online communications.

The majority of older non-users would like to learn, but on programmes that they perceived as being designed for people like themselves.

Essom (2006) identified low self-esteem and a lack of confidence as barriers to participating in learning. These are fundamental barriers to any learning and they need to be overcome if learners are to develop the skills and understanding required to use technology. However, there are examples of technology being used as an inducement for adults to take part in community-based provision and resulting in increased self-esteem and confidence. The DfES Laptop Initiative demonstrated the potential of ICT to motivate adults to return to learning (Clarke et al, 2003). Similar findings have been reported by several other investigations, such as the evaluation of the UK Online centres (Wyatt et al, 2003).

Many learners are interested in learning about ICT but do need to have the self-esteem and confidence to participate, although the prospect of learning about and through technology can be motivating.

Personal factors

Personal motivation, confidence and esteem are critical for successful learning. These can be developed through the course of study but if the potential learner lacks them, he or she may never even enrol. It is important to realise that for many people identified as socially or economically disadvantaged, simply enrolling is a major step. Once they have started the course, they need their decision to be reinforced by success and the increase in confidence that will bring. Without success there is a high probability that they will drop out of the programme.

About a third of all adults have not undertaken any form of learning since they left full-time education (Aldridge and Tuckett, 2006). This demonstrates that, for many adults, learning is not a natural or straightforward step to take.

Previous experience

A key factor in an individual's self-esteem and confidence as a learner is their previous experience in education and training. A poor experience can have an effect that lasts many decades. Many socially disadvantaged people have had poor education experiences which have convinced them that they cannot learn and so they are unwilling to participate. This can make them extremely reluctant to take part in anything associated with their previous poor experience, including their being unwilling to enter a formal institutional setting such as a college. However, people are often willing to participate in programmes based in community settings with which they are already familiar. Often called outreach, this has been shown to be a successful approach in reaching disadvantaged adults. Adults obviously do not associate outreach with their previous experiences.

Taking the initial step of enrolling can be stressful for a disadvantaged person. It is critical that their experience on the course quickly helps them to gain confidence, assuring them that they have made the right decision. Some activities that will often assist are:

- initial success even on minor matters;
- support and encouragement;
- opportunities to learn in their own context;
- realisation of their strengths.

Assessment is often associated with previous failure so it needs to be introduced with care and support. Tests are often a frightening experience for learners returning to education and training after many years. Initial assessment may be helpful in understanding the learner's needs and in helping you plan the course, but it can also be a source of considerable anxiety to them so needs to be approached with care and understanding.

REFLECTIVE TASK

Previous experience

Reflect on your own previous experience of education and training. Consider a new subject that you were starting to study. How did you feel? What helped you to succeed?

CASE STUDY – JAMES

James is teaching a class covering the basics of self-employment to a group of people who have recently been made redundant. He wants to emphasise the potential of ICT and the internet to help small businesses manage themselves, find useful information and market their services and products. He discovered in the first session that for the majority of the group this is their first education or training experience since leaving school. Many lack self-confidence in their ability to study, although they all have good skills to offer to customers and want to succeed as self-employed workers. He has begun to consult colleagues about what approaches he should take.

Discussion

There is a range of approaches that could be adopted such as:

1. It is important to start to build confidence, and success is a great enhancer of confidence. Devise a relevant activity at which everyone will succeed, such as locating information about tax and National Insurance on websites. Prepare the exercise to ensure that it is going to be effective. If learners work together in pairs then everyone will have a degree of support.

2. Build on the initial activity with a series of other activities that aim to develop self-esteem and confidence.
3. Treat the learners as adults and do not use methods they associate with their past experience, such as lecturing.
4. Discuss their needs and progress regularly with each person.
5. Use their purposes, context and language to build on.
6. Provide regular feedback on how they are progressing.

No method is guaranteed but remember that adult learners would not be in the class if they did not want to succeed.

Jargon

Jargon can be a barrier to most people. Technology has many new terms and also uses existing words in different ways. It can make people feel inadequate if they do not understand what is being discussed. This can make them decide they have chosen the wrong course or be reticent about asking questions. It can prove a formidable obstacle as it can be very difficult for people new to a course to admit that they do not understand what you mean. The solution is in your own approach. You must explain that:

- ICT has many new terms and that it is natural not to understand them. Everyone struggles with the language at first;
- explain each new term and familiar words used in a different way;
- provide handouts of terms explaining their meaning;
- help learners realise that not understanding jargon is experienced by everyone.

PRACTICAL TASK PRACTICAL TASK PRACTICAL TASK PRACTICAL TASK PRACTICAL TASK

Jargon

Create a short handout explaining the meaning of a variety of ICT terms that you think may confuse and discourage.

For example:

Memory
Storage
Router

Phobia

It is likely that a small minority of learners will have a fear of technology. This may be distrust of computers, an assumption that they are complex and place you at risk of being robbed or a belief that they corrupt. This can stem from experience or simply from observation. It may be easy to overcome or deeply embedded. In all cases, you need to treat it with care and respect the individual's views. The main factor influencing attitudes towards technology is experience. People who use ICT are more likely to have a positive attitude towards it than non-users (Dutton and Helsper, 2007). You need to provide opportunities for learners to use ICT in a safe and supportive environment so that their anxiety can slowly be reduced. A lack of knowledge is often the source of misconceptions, so discuss their views and help them to gain an understanding.

In some cases a small exposure to ICT will help learners to accept the technology and, in some cases, to become enthusiastic users. Other people, however, will need a longer period of support.

Institutional factors

A large college or training centre can often seem a daunting place for a learner who is not familiar with the environment. They are busy places and it can seem that everyone except the individual learner knows where to go and who to ask for. In some cases large educational providers have a number of sites with varying resources, so that support facilities may not be available at particular locations. Adult and community learning frequently operate in community locations where facilities may be limited to an individual tutor and what can be transported in a car. Institutional factors can limit you.

Methodologies

ICT is often taught in a stereotypical way, using workshop approaches with a focus on learning how to use a narrow range of applications such as word processing, spreadsheets and databases. Workshops can often be very effective in the development of ICT skills in that they allow learners to practise, work at their own pace and focus on their own needs. However, they can also leave you isolated with no immediate support; they may depend on handouts rather than human support and often assume a degree of self-confidence. Workshops need to be integrated with other methods (Clarke, 2006) to ensure success.

New learners need to be supported until they gain confidence. A confident learner with the basic technical skills may well benefit from a workshop in which they can concentrate on their own needs but the danger for new learners is that they will drop out or only learn what is covered in the handouts thus being unable to transfer their learning to new situations.

Many ICT programmes depend on following a scheme of work. These are often very good but do need to be used with flexibility and skill. Simply starting at Chapter 1 and working to the end will not relate to individual needs or existing skills. The schemes of work are frequently designed to allow learners to focus on particular subjects, so they can be used flexibly. Although ICT books are often written for learners, it is poor practice to rely only on them. The tutor is the most valued resource by almost all learners.

PRACTICAL TASK PRACTICAL TASK PRACTICAL TASK PRACTICAL TASK PRACTICAL TASK

Previous experience

Reflect on your own previous experience of learning to use technology. What did you find were the most effective approaches for you and why? What did you observe was the effect of these methods on your peers?

Support

The complexity, size and siting of the learning location can affect the availability of all types of support. A college covering a large city may well have many sites and specialist support staff could be based at a different location so that accessing them is not immediate. This could limit what you are able to do and in particular when you can carry it out. Technical support may be available but will probably prioritise work so that a routine task such as setting up equipment may be delayed if the college network has a fault. In Adult and Community Learning, technical support may simply not be available in community sites and so you are limited to your own skills.

The use of ICT in education and training has increased considerably over the last decade and many providers have specialist staff to support your use of technology. They have a variety of roles and titles. In adult and community learning, they are often known as E-guides with a role of providing mentoring and peer support although the details do vary. In colleges, they may be called ILT champions. The present situation has been created by different government initiatives linked to teacher training programmes. However, all providers have been free to integrate the role into their structures, with the result that there are considerable differences across the country. In addition to provider-based e-learning support, there are regional support centres (RSC) that support colleges and other providers. RSCs often organise networks of tutors and training programmes, offer advice and provide links to national developments.

PRACTICAL TASK PRACTICAL TASK PRACTICAL TASK PRACTICAL TASK PRACTICAL TASK

RSCs

Locate your RSC and identify what services and resources they can offer you.

Post-16 education and training is delivered in a vast range and variety of locations such as community centres, colleges, mobile learning centres, prisons, primary schools and a variety of other sites. Each will have a different approach to providing support and in many cases you will need to organise and plan access to support as it may not be immediately available.

Assessment

Initial assessment is a key part of education and training, providing you with an understanding of the needs of your learners and also their existing skills and knowledge. However, its value is dependent on the effectiveness of the assessment instruments and access to the results of the assessment. Because different approaches will have strengths and weaknesses, it is important to consider the approach to initial assessment and work with its strengths and overcome its weaknesses.

PRACTICAL TASK PRACTICAL TASK PRACTICAL TASK PRACTICAL TASK PRACTICAL TASK

Assessment

Find out what initial assessment is undertaken in your college or provider. Consider what its strengths and weaknesses are and how it could help you in preparing to teach.

Equipment

The post-16 education and training sector has made and is making a considerable investment in ICT equipment. However, access to and the availability of, hardware and software is not universal. For example, there are considerable differences between locations such as colleges and prison education departments. Security considerations are the first priority in prisons, so access to technology such as memory sticks or use of the internet may be limited or simply not available. BECTa (2007) reported that *schools and providers are still struggling with a range of technical and technology challenges*.

The BECTa (2007) report showed that in terms of computer–learner ratios across colleges, there had been a significant improvement over the last seven years. A majority of colleges had a computer for each five learners. However, there were some colleges with ratios of up to 11 learners for each computer. In other parts of the Post-16 sector, access to computers was less and the age and type of technology also varied considerably. Adult and Community Learning uses portable equipment extensively and has limited access to the internet due to community-based provision.

A key measure of the use of technology in learning has been developed by BECTa and is called e-maturity. This is defined as *the capability of institutions to resource, lead and manage technology-related change and to develop a workforce to utilise technology effectively to deliver technology-supported learning across the curriculum* (BECTa 2007). BECTa (2007) estimated that 25 per cent of colleges were e-mature in 2007.

A majority of colleges have now installed VLE to enhance their learning. A survey undertaken by OFSTED (2009) reported that there was considerable activity to develop VLEs but its impact at course level was small. Its use in the classroom depended on the teacher or trainer to exploit its possibilities. In locations where it was most effectively used, learners were assisted to reinforce their learning or to access materials that they had missed, but, in some cases it was simply a place to deposit documents.

BECTa (2006), in their annual review of ICT in education, reported that there were considerable differences in access to technology across the Post-16 sector, although there was steady improvement in access to technology over several years. Most education and training providers were using data projectors, electronic whiteboards and other equipment. However, this did not mean that there was universal access since across locations there were considerable differences. It would probably be necessary to book equipment or to teach in specific classrooms to guarantee access.

Teaching and learning factors

There are many teaching and learning factors that may limit a learner's ability to undertake the course successfully. ICT offers many ways to assist learning but if inappropriately used it can also be a barrier to progress. The first important step is to be aware of what is expected from the learner in terms of using technology. It is easy to consider that they are modest or minimal if you assume that:

- everyone has access to e-mail;
- everyone can send and receive text messages;
- all learners can search the internet.

If these are part of the course and the learners are not able to carry them out, they are a formidable barrier and many learners may simply drop out without even telling you why. You need to analyse carefully what is required of learners who undertake the course. Do not assume everyone can use ICT as well as yourself.

Analysis will show you the assumptions that have been made about the programme. You may need to adjust some of them or simply plan how you are going to help learners to develop their skills. Learners need to know what is expected of them so explain the ICT aspects and use it to motivate them. Many people are interested in improving their skills and will see the opportunities as added value.

The opportunities to develop ICT skills and knowledge embedded in the course need to be exploited, otherwise they will lose or fail to achieve their potential. A critical aspect of ICT is that it changes and develops continuously, therefore there is a need to be able to transfer skills to new situations. Transference is aided by the learners understanding what they are doing. It is often easy to prepare a handout, taking learners step-by-step through an ICT related task. This will enable them to undertake the course activity but is unlikely to result in understanding. At best, the learner will be able to learn by rote. A handout is useful to reinforce learning once understanding is established but it should not replace it.

ICT and e-learning

Although ICT is a curriculum area, it is also a means of supporting and delivering learning in a wide range of other subjects. It is possible to combine the two activities so that technology skills and knowledge are being developed while it is being used to support learning in another subject. However, this type of integration requires planning and careful preparation. The danger is that neither purpose will be achieved. It is important to know what your objectives for an activity are.

During the ICT Skill for Life pathfinder project, the development of the ITQ for Life and NIACE's embedding ICT with literacy and numeracy projects, efforts were made to map the ICT, numeracy and literacy skills for life standards against each other. The mapping demonstrated a 70 per cent overlap between ICT and literacy and a 40 per cent between ICT and numeracy standards. This shows substantial possibilities for the subjects to be integrated together for the benefit of the learner.

SCENARIO STUDY – WORD PROCESSING AND WRITING

Word processing is an excellent tool for helping learners to practice writing because they can be helped with spelling and grammar, can amend their writing without rewriting large sections and can produce a good copy through a printer so poor handwriting does not de-motivate. However, if their word processing skills are poor they may well be distracted by not knowing how to use a mouse, create blank lines, delete or many of the other functions that are useful once you understand them.

A focus on learning to use a word processor is likely to emphasise use of the mouse and keyboard skills, understanding functions such as backspace, delete, caps lock, scrolling and the various other functions. This is not going to help directly with writing.

Discussion

It is possible to blend the two activities together, not least because learners are often motivated to learn through the use of technology. You might begin with a focus on learning the basics of word processing, move on to writing and introduce more advanced functions step-by-step as the writing develops. In this way, both sets of skills are developed.

ICT provides a set of tools for the user to employ to meet their needs in a purposeful way. It can therefore help when choosing what products to buy by reading online reviews, communicate with family and friends through e-mail and keep family accounts on a spreadsheet. These are all useful purposes. Learners are motivated to learn how to use tools to achieve their purposes.

Technology can be used straightforwardly to assist learners to learn new skills and knowledge. That is, as part of an e-learning approach. It is not the direct intention of e-learning to develop the learners' technological skills. However, normally some understanding is gained even when it is used purely as e-learning. There are many e-learning approaches such as:

- webquest – asking individuals or groups of learners to analyse information on specific websites in order to carry out a task;
- digital cameras – to illustrate or record an activity or as part of a project;
- wiki – to work collaboratively to produce an agreed document.

In relation to literacy, language and numeracy there are a variety of approaches. These include:

- using websites to provide a wide range of reading content to meet the diverse needs and interests of learners;
- taking part in numerical games;
- using video cameras as part of projects to investigate issues (e.g. local transport);
- using podcasts to practise listening;
- using online learning resources (e.g. www.moneymatterstome.co.uk/) to provide specific experience;
- using voting systems to encourage participation and engagement.

NIACE have published a series of practical guides linking technology and e-learning to literacy, language and numeracy (Clarke et al, 2009b: Smith, 2008; Moss and Southwood, 2006). E-learning like any other educational method can be used inappropriately. This is often the result of poor understanding of e-learning by the teacher or trainer.

SCENARIO STUDY – USE OF INFORMATION ON THE WORLD WIDE WEB

The world wide web provides an enormous information resource that can assist people studying almost any subject. A group of people seeking to improve their literacy skills may well be offered the opportunity to search the internet for information that interests them. However, this type of open-ended task is unlikely to be very effective since it is vague and unrelated to a particular objective.

Discussion

The effective use of the information located on the world wide web is dependent on:

1. Identifying a defined objective for the task (e.g. locate reviews of digital cameras to determine which is the best buy for under £100).
2. Explaining to learners why they are undertaking the task – how it relates to their needs (e.g. practise reading reviews).
3. Providing support (e.g. working in small groups so peer support is available).
4. Offering feedback on what they achieved and the process they undertook.
5. Integrating the activity into the overall learning programme.

Your own attitude and personal confidence in respect to technology is likely to have a large influence on your learners. Many reviews of what learners' value in learning about ICT identifies the tutor as the most valuable resource available to them. If you indicate doubt about the value of using technology it will transfer to your learners in the same way that enthusiasm does. In a similar way if you are unable to use the technology available in the classroom such as electronic whiteboards then they will draw conclusions about your own ICT skills and understanding. It is important to prepare and plan your use of technology so that it works effectively. The impact of poor use will spread across several areas and not simply be linked to the specific task.

Many learners improve their ICT skills informally working at home or between sessions in learning centres. You can often assist this process by providing additional activities and exercises for them to work on. However, you do need to consider the learners' skills profiles. It is clear that many people have spiky technology profiles with expertise in one area not being matched to others. It is important to be aware of the profile of your learners so that you can develop appropriate activities.

A SUMMARY OF KEY POINTS

> Ofcom's Consumer Panel (2006) survey reported that a majority of older non-users of communication technologies would be interested in learning about them on programmes that they perceived as being designed for people like themselves.

> About a third of all adults have not undertaken any form of learning since they left full-time education (Aldridge and Tuckett, 2006).

> A key factor in an individual's self-esteem and confidence in themselves as learners is their previous experience in education and training.

> Jargon is a barrier to most people in that technology has many new terms and also uses existing words in different ways.

> A small minority of learners will have a fear of technology.

> A large college or training centre can often be a daunting place for a learner who is not familiar with the environment.

> ICT is often taught in a stereotypical way using workshop approaches with a focus on learning to use a narrow range of applications such as word processing, spreadsheets and databases.

> Workshops can often be inappropriately used to develop ICT skills.

> The complexity, size and location of the learning location can affect the availability of all types of support.

> The use of ICT in education and training has increased considerably over the last decade and many providers have specialist staff to support your use of technology.

> The value of initial assessment depends on the effectiveness of the approach and whether you have access to the results.

> Access to, and availability of, hardware and software will depend on your location and type of provider you are employed by.

> The BECTa (2007) report showed that in terms of computer-to-learner ratios across colleges there had been a significant improvement over the previous seven years but there were large differences across the sector.

> ICT offers many ways to assist learning but it also can be a barrier to progress if inappropriately used.

> The opportunities to develop ICT skills and knowledge embedded in the course need to be exploited otherwise they will be lost or fail to achieve their potential.

> ICT is both a curriculum subject and a means of supporting and delivering learning in a wide range of other subjects.

> It is possible to combine the two activities so that technology skills and knowledge are being developed while it is being used to support learning in another subject.

> The mapping of the ICT and literacy skills for life standards shows a 70 per cent overlap between them while mapping ICT and numeracy shows a 40 per cent overlap.

> The tutor's attitude and personal confidence in respect to technology is likely to have a large influence on learners.

> Many people have spiky technology profiles with expertise in one area not being matched to others. It is important to be aware of the skills profiles of your learners so that you can develop appropriate activities.

REFERENCES AND FURTHER READING REFERENCES AND FURTHER READING

Aldridge, F and Tuckett, A (2006) *The NIACE Survey on Adult participation in Learning: Green Shoots?* London: NIACE.

BECTa (2006) *The BECTa REVIEW 2006, Evidence on the progress ofg ICT in education.* Coventry: BECTa.

BECTa (2007) *Harnessing Technology Review: 2007, Summary report.* Coventry: BECTa.

Clarke, A, Reeve, A, Esson, J, Scott, J, Aldridge, F and Lindsay, K (2003) *Adult and Community Learning: Laptop Initiative Evaluation.* Leicester: DfES. NIACE.

Clarke, A (2006) *Teaching Adults ICT Skills. Exeter:* Learning Matters

Clarke, A, Essom, J and Faulkner, L (2009a) *ICT and literacy.* Leicester: NIACE

Clarke, A, Essom, J and Faulkner, L (2009b), *ICT and numeracy.* Leicester: NIACE

E-guides, (nd) [online]. Available at: excellence.qia.org.uk/page.aspx?o=135576 [accessed 20 January 2009].

Essom, J (2006) *Attracting and motivating learners with ICT: E-guidelines 7.* Leicester: NIACE.

Financial Literacy Resources (nd) [online]. Available at: www.moneymatterstome.co.uk/ [accessed 24 January 2009].

Mellar, H, Kambouri, M, Sanderson, M and Pavlov, V (2004) *ICT. and adult literacy, numeracy and ESOL.* London: National Research and Development Centre for adult literacy and numeracy.

Nance, B, Kambouri, M and Mellar, H (2007) *Using ICT.* Leicester: NIACE, London: NRDC

NIACE (2008) *ICT Skill for Life: Embedding ICT in Literacy and Numeracy.* Leicester: NIACE.

Ofcom Consumers Panel (2006) *Older People and Communications Technology.* London: Ofcom.

OFSTED (2009) *Virtual learning environments: an evaluation of their development in a sample of educational settings.* Manchester: Ofsted.

QCA (2007) *ICT Skill for Life Curriculum.* [online]. Available at: http://www.qca.org.uk/libraryAssets/media/skill_for_life_ict_curriculum_jan07.pdf [accessed 21 January 2009].

Regional Support Centres (nd) [online]. Available at: www.jisc.ac.uk/rsc [accessed 20 January 2009].

Smith, MP (2008) *Money Matters to me: A guide for adult learning practitioners.* Leicester: NIACE

Moss, M and Southwood, S (2006) *E-Learning for teaching ESOL.* Leicester: NIACE

Wyatt, J, Allison, S, Donoghue, D, Horton, P and Kearney, K (2003) *Evaluation of CMF funded UK online centres – final report, Hall Aitken.* London: Department for Education and Skills.

6
Communicating about ICT

This chapter will help you to:

- **be aware of methods and purposes of assessment in ICT;**
- **be aware of the role of communication in ICT;**
- **be aware of effective ways to communicate;**
- **understand what is meant by purposeful use of ICT;**
- **understand the essential characteristics of ICT;**
- **be aware of the ways learners develop ICT skills.**

Links to minimum core ICT

A2   Awareness of methods and purposes of assessment in ICT.
       Awareness of the role of communication in ICT.
       Awareness of effective ways to communicate.
       Understand what is meant by purposeful use of ICT.
       Understand the essential characteristics of ICT.
       Awareness of the ways learners develop ICT skills.

Links to LLUK Professional Standards

AK5.1 Ways to communicate and collaborate with colleagues and/or others to enhance learners' experience.
BP1.1 Establish a purposeful learning environment where learners feel safe, secure, confident and valued.
BP3.1 Communicate effectively and appropriately using different forms of language and media, including written, oral and non-verbal communication, and new and emerging technologies to enhance learning.
CK3.5 Ways to support learners in the use of new and emerging technologies in own specialist area.

Links to Certificate in Teaching in the Lifelong Learning Sector (CTLLS)

Unit 2 Planning and enabling learning.

Links to Diploma in Teaching in the Lifelong Learning Sector (DTLLS)

Unit 2 Planning and enabling learning.
Unit 3 Enabling learning and assessment.
Unit 4 Theories and principles for planning and enabling learning.

Introduction

The subject of ICT is rapidly changing and developing, having already made significant differences to the society in which we live. Developing ICT skills and knowledge is not a one-off in which acquiring a qualification by attending a single course will meet your lifelong needs. It is simply a starting point for a continuous process of development in which you strive to maintain and enhance your expertise.

ICT is also a wide subject with many different aspects, tools and approaches. You may only need to become competent in a relatively narrow area to meet your needs at any one time. However, a key factor is the ability to cope with change. New versions of software applications are continuously being launched so you need to be able to transfer your existing experience to them and then adapt to the new functions or facilities they offer.

New developments are often associated with new terminology meaning that communication is affected by the use of jargon or, in the case of ICT, the use of existing terms in new ways. The latter is potentially more challenging because the listener may be puzzled by the use of a familiar term in a different context. The potential for misunderstanding and confusion is clearly present.

While e-mail has certainly revolutionised the way business and society works, communication technology is more than just that. It is also instant messenger, video conferencing, Twitter, social networking and forums, names that are meaningless to some people.

ICT assessment

ICT assessment takes a variety of forms. In a range of ICT user qualifications, it is a practical test in which you are required to use your skills and understanding to carry out a task. This is often an activity you may need to undertake in a workplace such as:

- create a poster from a set of provided resources (e.g. images and text);
- write a business letter;
- send an e-mail;
- edit a digital photograph.

These are essentially tests in which you can apply the skills of using a range of designated applications in particular contexts. Because they are not contexts the learner has selected, they may not be relevant to their needs. The vocational aspects may well be suitable for people seeking to gain or retain employment but they are not relevant to an older, retired person who wants to use ICT to assist a hobby or another aspect of their personal life. A range of ICT qualifications for users have a vocational aspect and associated assessment.

The ICT Skill for Life and Functional Skills qualifications are based on standards that emphasise purposeful use in a range of contexts. The contexts for ICT Skill for Life are:

- citizen and community;
- economic activity, including paid and unpaid work;
- domestic and everyday life;
- leisure;
- education and training.

The ICT Functional Skills are very similar and cover:

- work – this includes unpaid voluntary activities;
- everyday life – such as leisure, family, children and household;
- education and training;
- community.

These are clearly very similar, and both aim to equip people with the skills to use ICT in all aspects of their lives. In both cases, probably the best way of assessing their skills is to ask for evidence that users are able to undertake purposeful tasks in a context of their choice. They would be free to select which application they wanted to use. This would be appropriate, since there is often a variety of applications that could be used for any particular task. This analysis would suggest a portfolio approach, probably electronic, since the learners may want to provide evidence in a range of formats. In practice, the assessment approach is described as test and task, where learners are asked to undertake a practical task and then to answer a series of questions. This method has been adopted due to the practical difficulties of administering large numbers of e-portfolios.

Users often have got spiky profiles of skills with exceptional skill in some areas and none in others (e.g. outstanding word processing skills but no experience of spreadsheets). Many jobs require a focused set of ICT skills and do not need the employee to be skilled and knowledgeable about all aspects of technology. Similarly students wanting to use ICT to aid their learning would want to develop a specific range of skills. The ICT sector skills council has realised that different employers and occupations require different mixes of ICT skills. In order to meet this need, they have developed a new vocational qualification called the ITQ.

REFLECTIVE TASK

Assessment experience

Consider your own experience of having your ICT skills and knowledge assessed. What form did the assessment take and did you feel it was an effective approach?

The ITQ is available at Levels 1, 2 and 3 but it allows learners to mix and match skills and knowledge from all levels to develop the required spiky profile for their occupation or employer. To support this approach, e-skills have developed a self-assessment tool (i.e. e-skills passport) that can be used by individuals, employers, teachers and trainers. This allows specific profiles to be developed and existing skill levels to be compared against it. Existing qualifications that are compatible with the ITQ standard can be linked to the passport to show learners' skill levels.

ITQ is an ICT qualification designed to be customised for any occupation or employer. NIACE, in partnership with e-skills with the support of BECTa, have been piloting an ITQ for teachers that is designed to provide them with the skills and knowledge they require.

ICT skills are essentially practical so probably the best approach to assessment is one that requires evidence that ICT can be used to carry out appropriate purposeful tasks. This should involve the learner being able to select the tool to undertake the activity and to explain why it is the most suitable. Apart from the actual skill of using a tool in a purposeful way, there is a range of associated skills and knowledge that are required to get the desired results, such as:

- information literacy so you can judge the quality and fitness for purpose of information located through searching;
- design skills to create content;
- literacy and numeracy skills.

Many disadvantaged people have neither access to technology nor the skills to use it effectively. They may also have had poor experiences of education and training. This may leave them reluctant to be assessed and very anxious of the assessment process. Assessment methods based on gathering evidence that is a by-product of learning to develop a portfolio are often new to disadvantaged learners and those with little previous experiences of being tested. It is important to be aware that assessment can be a negative process for many people and you should work towards overcoming the fears it generates.

SCENARIO STUDY – ON THE WORLD WIDE WEB

Judging Information

A key issue for any user of the world wide web is to judge the quality of the information that is presented on websites. Anyone can establish a website and present information on any topic they desire. There are not overarching quality assurance standards that everyone must follow. So it is essentially 'user beware'. How can you distinguish between different sources?

Discussion

It is not easy and even the most experienced user of the world wide web makes mistakes and misjudges content. However, some straightforward approaches are:

1. Who owns the websites? Are they appropriate for the type of information displayed?
2. How often has the website been updated? A poorly maintained site may suggest inaccurate information.
3. What websites are linked to and from the site?
4. Is the information repeated on other sites to confirm its accuracy?

The information on an individual's website might be no more than personal opinion, but if that individual is a world authority on the subject then it may provide considerable insight into the issues.

Communication

Technology has changed the way that we communicate over the last 20 years. The use of text messages, e-mail, wikis and all the other forms of communication technology now enable you to communicate continuously and immediately. While two decades ago communication was occasional and involved a delay (e.g. the time for a letter to be sent and another to be returned) it is now a normal everyday sight to see people texting or sending e-mails from mobile devices in the street. Individuals send e-mails from laptops on trains and wireless hotspots are now wide-spread. Nevertheless, this availability of communication does not mean that it is effective.

E-mail and many other forms of communication technology need to be used in the right way. An e-mail message has many strengths.

- It is easy to send a message to one person or many.
- It is almost instantaneous.
- Replies contain the original message.
- Messages can be forwarded to other people.
- It is asynchronous, so people read the messages when it is most convenient for them.
- It is possible to have a multi-way discussion with several people.

These are real strengths of e-mail, but there are also weaknesses.

- Informal and short messages predominate so misunderstandings are common.
- It is too easy to respond quickly to a misunderstanding and thus turn it into an argument.

To use e-mail effectively for communication needs care and consideration. Figures 6.1, 6.2 and 6.3 compare ways of sending and responding to a message. Figure 6.1 illustrates a simple message that is short and informal but clearly greets the intended recipient and closes the message. Long messages are rarer and perhaps because of this are often regarded negatively by recipients.

Figure 6.2 shows a reply that integrates the original message into the response to try to show links but this needs to be done carefully to avoid confusion. Figure 6.3 separates out the same reply and so requires the reader to be aware of the original message. Both can be used effectively but do need different approaches to communication.

Hi Keith

I was considering how to organise the workshop on judging the quality of information located through a search engine. This is an important topic but many people do little more than enter the first term that comes into their head into a search engine and accept whatever the top 10 hits generated say.

What do you think we should include?

Best Wishes

Sheila

Figure 6.1 E-mail message

Dear Sheila

Hi Keith

I was considering how to organise the workshop on judging the quality of information located through a search engine.

It is very easy for anyone to set up a website and present their personal views as facts so learners need to know how to judge them.

This is an important topic.

People do not use search engines effectively. They rarely employ any of the advanced search functions and are too easily satisfied with the results. They should explore and compare outcomes.

But many people do little more than enter the first term that comes into their head into a search engine and accept whatever the top 10 hits generated say.

What do you think we should include?

I would suggest that we include: advanced search functions, basics of judging different websites and some information literacy techniques. It needs to be practical and give plenty of examples.

Best Wishes

Sheila

Cheers

Keith

Figure 6.2 Integrating a reply to an e-mail

> Dear Sheila
>
> It is very easy for anyone to set up a website and present their personal views as facts so learners need to know how to judge them.
>
> People do not use search engines effectively. They rarely employ any of the advanced search functions and are too easily satisfied with the results. They should explore and compare outcomes.
>
> I would suggest that we include: advanced search functions, basics of judging different websites and some information literacy techniques. It needs to be practical and give plenty of examples.
>
> Cheers
>
> Keith

Figure 6.3 Replying with a new message

REFLECTIVE TASK

E-mail

Consider your preferred ways of sending and replying to e-mails. How often are your messages misunderstood? Have you ever had an argument by e-mail without meaning to do so?

E-mail is not only used to send messages to particular individuals but also to provide a means for groups of people to discuss topics or share ideas. E-mail forums are widely used in business and education, enabling groups to meet and debate.

E-mail is only one way of communicating using technology. There are also text messages, which are limited to 160 characters and are widely used, with people sending many each day. There are billions of text message users around the globe sending billions of messages. Although limited by the number of characters, it is the most used and popular means of communicating and is very effective. The vast majority of people have a mobile phone and thus access to text messages. Many educational providers use texts to inform learners about changes to courses, teachers being ill, to remind them of assessment dates and any other features of the course.

The limited number of characters has led to the use of abbreviations to allow longer messages to be sent.

For example:

4 – for

U – you

Some people text continuously wherever they are – in the bus, in class, in a meeting and they seem to be able to do so in parallel with other activities.

Twitter messages are similar to texts in that they have a limited number of characters that can appear in any messages. The concept differs in that users broadcast what they are doing through messages to other users who follow particular people. This may seem a rather narrow form of communication but it is very popular and helps to create communities of interest. Twitter has been used to allow a form of shadowing in which a learner can gain an understanding of what is involved in particular jobs and tasks.

Instant messaging is different from e-mail in that it is a form of synchronous text communication (i.e. live or real time communication where both parties in the exchange are available at the same time). Its strength, wherein it is a real time method, is also its weakness because participants living in different parts of the world are in different time zones, making communication difficult to arrange. Another real time communication method is Skype, which is essentially having a telephone conversation using the internet. It is a cheap method if you have a broadband connection and a Skype handset.

Video conferencing is another real time communication technology with the important difference being that you can see and speak with the other party. It is also not limited to individuals in that more than one person can take part at each end. It can take various forms from a simple camera added to a personal computer allowing two people to talk, to a professional system in which a meeting involving many people can take place.

There are many communication technologies and more will probably emerge. It is common for different technologies to be used in parallel such as e-mail forums that provide instant messaging so that users who happen to visit the site simultaneously have the option to communicate in real time.

Communication technologies have changed and will probably continue to change the way society operates. People have taken enthusiastically to many of them and you are at a disadvantage if you are unable to participate.

Purposeful use

Clarke (2007) provides a range of examples and explanations of the purposeful use of ICT. He emphasises that purposeful use is about using ICT tools to meet the needs of the user. It is not about learning to use ICT applications for their own sake but rather to achieve objectives and goals. Some examples, using the five contexts of ICT Skill for Life, are given below:

1. Citizen and Community – for example, to send an e-mail to your MP expressing your views about a government policy, in order to gain their support.
2. Economic activity, including paid and unpaid work – for example, to keep financial records.
3. Domestic and everyday life – for example, to design your new kitchen.
4. Leisure – for example, to check what is playing at the local theatre.
5. Education and training – for example, to order a textbook for a course you are undertaking.

PRACTICAL TASK PRACTICAL TASK PRACTICAL TASK PRACTICAL TASK PRACTICAL TASK

Purposeful

Consider the five contexts for ICT Skill for Life. Decide whether tasks that you have undertaken or will undertake in all contexts are purposeful.

The ICT Skill for Life Curriculum document (QCA, nda) provides many examples of purposeful use at all levels from Entry Level 1 to Level 2. The ICT Skill for Life standards (QCA, ndb) in its introduction to the standards offers an insight into the meaning of purposeful. It emphasises the fundamental role that ICT plays in adult life in individual, community and employment activities. Individuals will want to use ICT to meet their needs in the contexts that are relevant to them. Each person is different, therefore purpose relates to individual need. This may sound very obvious, but the traditional approach to teaching ICT tends to emphasis learning to use a standard range of applications, such as word processing, spreadsheets, e-mail and presentation software. These were taught almost as pure subjects with little personal context except perhaps that provided by the assessment which was often a general vocational one. Many teachers and trainers realised that they could motivate learners by encouraging them to suggest a task they could undertake to practise using the application, but this was always limited by the assessment required.

The ICT skills functional standards provide a summary interpretation in, *learners use a range of ICT tools in a purposeful way to tackle questions, solve problems and create ideas and solutions of value in a range of contexts, and in other areas of learning, work and life*. This provides a clear view of purpose with a focus on use in a specific context to meet a need.

REFLECTIVE TASK

Experience

Consider your own experience of attending ICT training and educational sessions. What emphasis was provided – a purposeful one or one centred on using a particular application? What would have been the best approach for you?

Essential characteristics

The danger of a section called 'essential characteristics' of ICT is that you merely compile a list of ICT applications. Because ICT is a set of tools that allow you to undertake tasks and meet your needs, it is also important to consider the nature of the tasks that you would use ICT to fulfil. The ICT Skill for Life standard is focused on combining skills for and knowledge of using ICT hardware and software with activities or purposes. It is divided into three themes which are:

- using ICT systems;
- finding and exchanging information;
- developing and presenting information.

These themes are further broken down into sections and these provide many of the essential characteristics of ICT. The standard is presented at five levels from Entry Level 1 to Level 2, in other words, from beginner to competent user. The emphasis at Level 2 is on the user being able to work independently and handle complex tasks. These are also characteristics of using ICT. The sections are:

1. Using ICT systems
   - Using a computer and input devices.
   - Using software applications.

- Interacting with and through the interface.
- Using portable storage devices.
- Managing files and folders.
- Customising computer settings.
- Safe and secure working.
2. Finding and exchanging information
    - Identifying and using sources of information.
    - Searching for and locating information.
    - Navigating the world wide web.
    - Using communication technology.
    - Understanding copyright and other constraints.
3. Developing and presenting information
    - Entering and editing information.
    - Checking content and correcting errors.
    - Sorting information.
    - Manipulating and formatting presentation of information.
    - Presenting information.
    - Reviewing effectiveness of outcome.

The standard emphasises fit-for-purpose choices and approaches, with the user able to select the most appropriate method.

There are also some other important characteristics of ICT. The first is that it is a subject continuously changing with new applications, new versions of established applications and new developments. Currently, the growth in the use of blogs, wikis and other types of system is turning the world wide web from a resource where you locate and read information to one in which much of the content is produced by users. In parallel, cloud computing, in which applications are not installed on a computer but accessed from websites so that you can work anywhere in the world, is beginning to become available. This lends itself to collaborative working, since content is also stored online and can be shared with other users. These are just a couple of examples of new developments. More will follow and this pace of change is an essential characteristic of ICT. Users need to develop their skills and knowledge regularly or run the risk of becoming out of date. Continuous development is essential.

There are several related areas that influence the effective use of ICT for a purpose such as:

- information and media literacy – judging the quality and appropriateness of information;
- literacy – the main communication technologies are based on written messages;
- numeracy – many applications and methods (e.g. searching) assume understanding of mathematics;
- study skills – if the user is also an online or e-learner.

Because there are normally many alternative approaches to undertaking a task, it is important that users are able to make choices in order to achieve the desired outcome effectively. The ability to transfer previous experience to new activities and applications is vital.

Developing ICT skills

ICT is a practical subject and it requires practice to develop the required skills. However, it also needs to be understood, rather than merely 'understand' by rote learning.

Understanding helps users to solve problems and overcome difficulties. Whereas you can operate a television without ever knowing what happens inside the set, ICT is assisted by knowing something about the way a computer operates and how the internet works. This does not mean that you need to be able to build a computer but understanding the difference between, say, random access memory and storage is useful. Users need to be able to safeguard their systems from virus and spyware attack and to be able to navigate websites.

Many ICT users have taught themselves and have never attended a course or gained a qualification. Many courses realise that practice between the face-to-face sessions is important and so provide assistance in the form of tasks and activities to be undertaken outside the classroom. This is important but often learners need assistance, so support is vital. Peer or group support can often be very effective in overcoming difficulties. You should develop a learning environment that encourages mutual support through paired tasks or group work. It is often a mistake to provide a stream of individual tasks. Individual practice is important but so are paired and group activities. A balance and variety of teaching methods is needed so that the different learning preferences of individual learners are assisted.

REFLECTIVE TASK

Own learning

Consider some aspects of ICT skills and knowledge that you developed independently. What were the strengths and weaknesses of the approach. Now consider some skills that you gained through an educational or training course. Again, what were its strengths and weaknesses?

Compare and contrast the approaches.

Clarke (2006), discussing how ICT should be taught to adult learners, emphasises the need for the full range of methods to be employed so as to allow learners choice. People have a range of learning styles and preferences and the risk is that by focusing on some, you will isolate learners with other preferences. This can lead to poor retention rates.

ICT is a subject in which confidence is key. Learners will gain from being able to explore, try new applications and experiment. To be able to investigate the technological world, you need confidence as well as the ability to transfer your existing experience to the new situations. Motivation is clearly at the core of this willingness to try new things and this comes from using ICT to undertake relevant tasks. The activities must be purposeful and meet the learners' needs and interests.

A SUMMARY OF KEY POINTS

> To maintain ICT skills and knowledge requires a continuous process of development.

> A key factor is learning to cope with change.

> Communication technology is more than e-mail (e.g. instant messenger, video conferencing, Twitter, social networking and forums).

> ICT assessment takes a variety of forms (e.g. a practical test, a portfolio of evidence and questions).

> The ICT Skill for Life and Functional Skills qualifications emphasise purposeful use in a range of contexts.

> Users often have spiky profiles of skills, with exceptional skill in some areas and none in others.

> The ITQ is available at Levels 1, 2 and 3, but it allows learners to mix and match skills and knowledge from all levels in order to develop the required spiky profile for their occupation or employer.

> In addition to the actual skill of using a tool in a purposeful way, there is a range of associated skills and knowledge (e.g. information literacy).

> The use of text messages, e-mail, wikis and all the other forms of communication technology now allow you to communicate continuously and immediately.

> E-mail has both strengths and weaknesses.

> Purposeful use is about using ICT tools to meet the needs of the user.

> The essential characteristics of ICT are more than just using ICT tools and systems. They include using the ICT tools to find, exchange, develop and present information.

> ICT is a practical subject and requires practice to develop the required skills. However, understanding something of the workings of a computer helps users to solve problems and overcome difficulties.

> ICT should be taught using the full range of methods to provide for different learning styles and preferences.

> Learners will gain confidence in ICT from being able to explore, try new applications and experiment.

REFERENCES AND FURTHER READING REFERENCES AND FURTHER READING

Clarke, A (2006) *Teaching Adults ICT Skills.* Exeter: Learning Matters.

E-skills Passport (nd) [online]. Available at: www.e-skillspassport.com/ [accessed 25 January 2009].

ITQ (nd) [online]. Available at: itq.e-skills.com/ [accessed 25 January 2009].

QCA (nda) *Skill for Life: ICT Curriculum* [online]. Available at www.qca.org.uk/qca_4560.aspx [accessed 25 January 2009].

QCA (ndb) *Skill for Life: ICT Curriculum* [online]. Available at www.qca.org.uk/qca_4560.aspx [accessed 25 January 2009].

ICT *Functional Skills* (nd) [online]. Available at: curriculum.qca.org.uk/key-stages-3-and4/subjects/ict/keystage4/Functional_skills_in_the_revised_programme_of_study_for_ICT.aspx [accessed 25 January 2009].

7
Personal ICT skills: communication

This chapter will help you to:

- communicate with/about ICT in a manner that supports open discussion;
- be able to assess your own, and others' understanding, including:
  - communicating ICT concepts clearly and effectively;
  - using the language of ICT accurately.
- be able to recognise differences in language needs; formulate and provide appropriate responses and recognise appropriate use of communication about/with ICT by others;
- be able to use language and other forms of representation to:
  - reinforce oral communication of ICT concepts and skills;
  - check how well the information is received;
  - support the understanding of those listening.

Links to minimum core ICT
B   Personal ICT Skills.

Communicate with/about ICT in a manner that supports open discussion.

Assess your own, and others' understanding, communicate ICT concepts clearly and effectively and use the language of ICT accurately.

Recognise differences in language needs; formulate and provide appropriate responses and recognise appropriate use of communication about/with ICT by others.

Use language and other forms of representation to reinforce oral communication of ICT concepts and skills, check how well the information is received and support the understanding of those listening.

Links to LLUK Professional Standards
AK4.2 The impact of own practice on individuals and their learning.

AK5.1 Ways to communicate and collaborate with colleagues and/or others to enhance learners' experience.

BP3.1 Communicate effectively and appropriately using different forms of language and media, including written, oral and non-verbal communication, and new and emerging technologies to enhance learning.

CK3.5 Ways to support learners in the use of new and emerging technologies in own specialist area.

CP 3.5 Make appropriate use of, and promote the benefits of new and emerging technologies.

Links to Certificate in Teaching in the Lifelong Learning Sector (CTLLS)
Unit 2 Planning and enabling learning.

Links to Diploma in Teaching in the Lifelong Learning Sector (DTLLS)
Unit 2 Planning and enabling learning.

Unit 3 Enabling learning and assessment.

Unit 4 Theories and principles for planning and enabling learning.

Introduction

Communication is the vital component in teaching and training. Communication technologies are central to the use of technology in society and in e-learning. It is therefore essential that you have the skills and understanding to use communication technology effectively in your teaching and professional life. In addition, you need to be able to communicate about ICT which can be a challenge, since not only does ICT use specific jargon and terms but also gives new meanings to existing words and phrases.

For example:

Download and upload are technical terms relating to the transfer of content from and to websites.

Drive – in ICT this refers to a storage location but in general relates to driving a car.

Assessing understanding

This section covers both assessing your own understanding and that of other people. It is important since it will enable you to assist your learners by asking them to undertake tasks that are appropriate, to avoid patronising them and to help you provide the necessary assistance to them. It involves the ability to communicate ICT concepts clearly and effectively, using the ICT language accurately.

The DfES Standards Unit (2005) identified three problems with using the language of ICT. These were:

* ICT uses lots of words inconsistently and interchangeably;
* ICT uses familiar words in an unfamiliar way;
* ICT has a technical vocabulary.

The Standards Unit and the subject coaches programme developed material to address ICT language and these are available through the Excellence Gateway website or directly through the subject learning coaches site (http://www.subjectlearningcoach.net/index.aspx).

PRACTICAL TASK PRACTICAL TASK PRACTICAL TASK PRACTICAL TASK PRACTICAL TASK

Language

Consider the ICT language that you use and try to identify the three groups of terms that the Standards Unit identified as problems, that is:

1. Words used interchangeably and inconsistently.
2. Familiar words used in unfamiliar ways.
3. ICT technical terms.

In using the language of ICT there are two factors that you need to consider:

1. Using the language correctly.
2. Learners' understanding of the terms.

Even if you are correctly using ICT terms it can still cause confusion and misunderstanding if your learners are unfamiliar with the vocabulary or simply think you mean the word as it appears in general English (e.g. application). It is vital that your use of the language matches the learners' understanding. A straightforward approach for you to adopt is to be consistent in your own use of terms and avoid using interchangeable ones. In addition, explain each new term that you introduce and explain familiar words that have a new meaning in ICT.

CASE STUDY – ADULT LEARNERS' ICT LANGUAGE

Mike is concerned that a group of adult learners, with whom he wants to use e-learning methods to enhance their learning, do not have a sufficient understanding of ICT terms. Misunderstanding is preventing the effective use of ICT in the course. He decides to research what is available to help him and discovers a pack of materials produced by the DfES Standards Unit. Its purpose is to help ICT teachers and trainers improve the teaching and learning of ICT. Amongst the pack are some practical exercises to assist with overcoming the problems associated with ICT language.

Discussion

The Standards Unit exercises cover:

1. A version of the card game Snap in which learners are asked to match words that can be used interchangeably, such as screen and monitor.

2. Getting learners to complete a worksheet that gives a variety of terms with an example of how they are used in ICT, then asking them to give a brief example of the words' use in everyday communication.

3. Giving examples of how learners describe ICT when they do not know the correct terms (e.g. 'the radio is not working' – this may mean that they cannot establish a wireless connection) and encouraging a discussion of the problems that it causes.

Each of the activities could be used to discuss the issues and encourage learners to seek assistance from the teacher, trainer and peers.

The learning atmosphere in the classroom can help substantially in overcoming the problems that ICT language causes. A climate in which learners feel comfortable asking for help from you or their peers is vital in ensuring that language does not become a barrier. Learners need to feel that it is natural to seek support and ask the meaning of unfamiliar terms without embarrassment. This enables you to assess the understanding and skills of your learners. The Standard Unit exercises can also provide a focus for assessment and encourage discussion of the issues.

In 2003, the Department for Innovation, Universities and Skills undertook a national survey of people's awareness and practical skills in relation to ICT. The survey showed a reasonable level of awareness of ICT applications and terminology with 50 per cent of the sample achieving Level 2 or above in the test. In contrast, the associated practical skills were often poorer in that only 10 per cent of the sample had practical skills at Level 2 or above. In addition, 15 per cent had never used a computer. Dutton and Helsper (2007) reported that 32 per cent of people in Britain had never used a computer, based on their survey of internet use in Britain. These surveys show that it is dangerous to assume that knowledge of ICT terminology is linked to similar practical skills. It may well not be and practical skills may be significantly poorer. You need to assess practical skills in addition to language.

Your own needs

It is important to be aware of your own knowledge and skills of ICT communication.

Needs

Consider your role and how you will need to use communication technology in your teaching and professional life. How would you assess your skills and knowledge and prioritise the areas that you would need to develop. Table 7.1 provides a structure for the assessment.

Table 7.1 provides a means of analysing your personal ICT communication skills in relation to the ICT minimum core. The columns ICT minimum core areas and key areas present the standard. In the Skills and understanding column you should indicate your current knowledge and skills and in the Activity column those actions that could help you develop your skills in that area. The final step is to use the last column, Priority, to show how important that area is to your development.

ICT minimum core areas	Key areas	Skills and understanding	Activity	Priority
To communicate with/about ICT in a manner that supports open discussion				
To be able to assess your own and others' understanding	Communicating ICT concepts clearly and effectively			
	Using the language of ICT accurately			
To be able to recognise differences in language needs; formulate and provide appropriate responses and recognise appropriate use of communication about/with ICT by others				

Table 7.1 ICT communication skills analysis

ICT minimum core areas	Key areas	Skills and understanding	Activity	Priority
To be able to use language and other forms of representation	Reinforce oral communication of ICT concepts and skills			
	Check how well the information is received.			
	Support the understanding of those listening			

Table 7.1 ICT communication skills analysis

Open discussion

Communication technology is already used regularly to communicate to learners. It can simply be used as a means of reinforcing administration communication such as text messages to remind students that some facilities will not be available or that new options are available. This is normally undertaken in addition to notices being posted on display boards or letters sent to learners' homes. E-mail is equally widely employed to assist the communication between the education or training provider, tutors and learners. Many providers have established e-mail forums in which learners and tutors can discuss issues between or in place of face-to-face sessions. These are often effective in collaborative group work.

Online collaboration does not simply happen because you provide a technological means for people to communicate. It requires:

- a focus for collaboration;
- adequate time for the activity;
- flexibility so that learners have sufficient freedom to contribute when they are able;
- support for you to motivate the group and assist them overcome any problems.

Forum groups can provide a means of allowing equal opportunities for everyone to contribute. They can overcome the barrier that quiet or reticent learners often feel inhibited by more vocal peers. Online communication allows the learner to consider their contribution and to make it when they are ready. Your role is to encourage contributions and ensure that they are made in ways that do not inhibit other people.

E-mails are often short informal documents and have the potential to be misunderstood. This can lead to quick responses that can generate arguments. It is therefore important to provide a structure for online communication that keeps control of the environment while encouraging open discussion.

REFLECTIVE TASK

Good manners

Consider your own experience of e-mail messages that have annoyed you and how you have reacted to them. What lessons have you learnt about effective communication?

Netiquette

An effective way of providing a structure for open discussion is to agree a set of principles to govern the communication. This is often called netiquette. Clarke (2008) suggests
the following principles:

- Never be offensive or respond with anger to a message;
- Treat everyone with respect;
- Don't forward chain messages or send spam;
- Don't use all capitals in your messages as it can be viewed as the equivalent of shouting;
- Respect people's messages (e.g. don't copy messages to new recipients without
  permission);
- Remember humour is difficult to communicate and can be easily misunderstood.

It often useful to ask the group to agree their own set of principles. They will then have
ownership of them and be more likely to follow them.

Practical issues

Effective communication needs to be clear and free from errors. In this way recipients
will not misunderstand the messages and be able to respond accurately. This is not easy
to achieve and requires that you ask for feedback from your learners and peers so that
you are able to make changes and improve your communication. ICT provides many
functions that can assist your communication including:

- spelling and grammar checkers;
- print preview to allow you to check documents before they are produced;
- version control so that you are aware of the latest version of a document;
- a range of fonts and character sizes;
- colour;
- embolden, underline and use of italics for emphasis;
- borders;
- bullet points;
- line spacing.

The danger is that if these functions are over used they will distract the readers from the
content. The key is to use them systematically and consistently.

For example:

Use a different font and character size for headings so they are emphasised.

Use colours systematically – red for assessment information, blue for feedback and
black for information so that the reader can identify the type of information.

Consistency of presentation is often key to effective communication. Learners are then
able to realise that handouts and worksheets are always laid out in the same way so they
can find information in a straightforward way and will not miss key points. There are
many conventions for the presentation of documents so that you need to follow them if
they are appropriate in your subject.

Communication technology

It is important that your own skills of using technology to communicate are developed so
that you are able to use e-mail or other approaches effectively. This involves not only

composing and sending messages but also saving and managing them and maintaining an address book of contacts. The basics required are:

- reading and writing messages;
- replying to e-mail or other communications;
- forwarding messages;
- sending and opening attachments;
- completing e-mail template (e.g. from, to, cc, bcc, subject and content).

In addition you need to have experience of participating in forums, e-portfolios, blogs and wikis. These all require different styles and approaches to communication.

For example:

Blogs are often used to reflect on events and issues so need a reflective style of communication.

Wikis are a collaborative form of communication in which you edit other participants' contributions as well as adding your own input.

E-portfolio communications are often related to providing feedback on work undertaken by the learner so you are aiming to provide constructive comments to assist their learning.

PRACTICAL TASK PRACTICAL TASK PRACTICAL TASK PRACTICAL TASK PRACTICAL TASK

Blog

Visit a variety of educational blogs and consider the different communication styles that are used. Identify approaches that you feel are effective and consider why they are appropriate.

PRACTICAL TASK PRACTICAL TASK PRACTICAL TASK PRACTICAL TASK PRACTICAL TASK

Wikis

Visit a variety of educational wikis and consider the different communication styles that are used. Identify approaches that you feel are effective and consider why they are appropriate.

Google provides free access to Blogger, a system for the creation of blogs. Figure 7.1 illustrates Blogger.

Management of information

The management of your files and communications may seem a drab and unimportant set of tasks but they are vital to good communication. Technology provides the tools for personal productivity but they are wasted without organisation.

You need to be able to create a structure of folders and sub-folders to store your files so that you are able to quickly locate specific files (e.g. e-mail messages or attachments). This is often important if you are communicating with a large number of learners. It is important to be able to review previous messages before responding. E-mail systems (e.g. Microsoft Outlook) provide the functions to store messages, maintain address books of contacts and manage the inbox.

Figure 7.1 Blogger

Differences in language

The language of ICT is now a part of everyday communications. It forms part of the literacy standards that every person needs to function in a modern society. Many people have problems with literacy such as poor spelling and grammar, a limited vocabulary, little understanding of punctuation or a combination of different factors. This will influence their ability to understand communication about ICT. You need to be aware of the differences in language skills and needs between learners so that you can tailor your approach for each person. It is important to be able to recognise the differences in language needs between learners and develop appropriate responses.

ICT provides support for learners with different language needs through the provision of:

- spelling and grammar checkers – these can be used after composing a document or during the process;
- thesaurus – so that alternative words can be selected.

These functions support learners by providing them with choices (e.g. spell checkers only indicate a possible error the learner needs to decide) so that they have to develop an understanding of language.

Use of language

ICT is a practical subject so that simply explaining a concept, approach or a piece of hardware without showing or demonstrating it is unlikely to be completely effective. Communication that combines a demonstration with a verbal explanation is probably going to be the most effective method. Technology provides the means to produce effective demonstrations using video projectors so that a whole class of learners are able to see the screen while listening to your explanation. However, the exception is deaf or partially hearing learners when you should not speak and demonstrate at the same time.

A whole-class demonstration can be used to encourage a discussion about the topic and thus assist you to assess the overall understanding of the class. The group can ask questions and in a whole-class setting everyone can benefit from the answers. An alternative to a teacher presentation is to ask learners to prepare and carry out a demonstration for their peers. This is often very effective in that they will gain understanding not only of the task but also of how to present it to others.

REFLECTIVE TASK

REFLECTIVE TASK

Reflect on your own experience of listening to explanations of ICT concepts. What did you find the most and least effective approaches?

It is possible to capture a demonstration using software such as Camtasia Studio. This allows the learners to review the demonstration later so that they can consider the different aspects and stop and start the presentation. Your explanation is captured as well as the demonstration so learners can listen to your explanation as they watch the demonstration. There are a variety of capture products available and your employer may well have access to them.

Capturing demonstrations provides the means of developing a library of different presentations so that you can use them to help specific learners who may be struggling with particular ICT approaches or methods.

Obviously it is not simply about communicating effectively; it is also how much understanding that the listeners gain while listening to your presentation. You need to check that they have understood. The best way is probably to ask them to undertake a task that covers the content of the presentation. You can then observe their efforts and be able to check that they have understood. The feedback that you gain through observation is very valuable since you can often identify weaknesses in your demonstration and explanation and correct them.

To reinforce the task it can be supported with a handout that contains a series of screen captures so that learners have visual clues to assist their memory of the demonstration. There are many screen capture utilities (e.g. Paint Shop Pro).

This approach can be summarised as:

- show – demonstrate the ICT concept;
- tell – explain step by step;
- do – ask the learners to undertake an appropriate task;
- feedback – improve the demonstration and explanation;
- capture – provide a video and audio pack for review and to assist individual learners.

CASE STUDY – ALISON – E-MAIL FORUM

Alison was a science teacher and wanted to use an e-mail forum with her classes so that they could continue to discuss topics between sessions and provide each other with mutual support. Her students were quite technically literate but had not used a forum for group work or communication. She was considering how to introduce them to the environment so that they gained confidence and could quickly to start to communicate.

Discussion

She decided to:

1. Ask each learner to introduce themselves online so that everyone could practise the basics of sending a message.
2. Ask each learner to read a short paper about a topic and then to submit their views about it to the forum and then discuss it. In this way they could slowly be introduced to online discussion.
3. Actively support the discussion by welcoming contributions so that learners did not feel threatened but supported by the process.
4. Communicate outside the forum with learners who seemed reluctant to participate to encourage them to send messages.

A SUMMARY OF KEY POINTS

> DfES Standards Unit (2005) identified three problems with using the language of ICT: using words inconsistently and interchangeably; using familiar words in an unfamiliar way; and technical terms.

> You need to be consistent in your own use of terms, avoid using interchangeable terms and explain each new term.

> Learners need to feel that it is natural to seek support and ask the meaning of unfamiliar terms without embarrassment.

> The Department for Innovation, Universities and Skills national survey in 2003 showed a reasonable level of awareness of ICT applications and terminology but poor practical skills.

> Dutton and Helsper (2007) reported that 32 per cent of people in Britain had never used a computer.

> It is important to be aware of your own knowledge and skills of ICT communication.

> Communication technology is already used regularly to communicate to learners (e.g. text messages, e-mail, forums, blogs, wikis, e-portfolios, etc).

> Netiquette is an agreed set of principles to govern the communication.

> Consistency of presentation is often key to effective communication.

> The management of your files and communications is vital to good communication.

> Learners' literacy skills will influence their ability to understand communications about ICT.

> ICT also provides support for learners with different language needs through the provision of spelling and grammar checkers and a thesaurus.

> Communication that combines a demonstration with a verbal explanation is probably going to be the most effective method.

REFERENCES AND FURTHER READING REFERENCES AND FURTHER READING

Clarke, A (2008) *E-learning Skills,* second edition. Basingstoke: Palgrave Macmillan.
Department for Innovation, Universities and Skills (2003) *The Skills for Life survey: A national needs and impact survey of literacy, numeracy and ICT skills* [online]. Avilable at: www.dcsf.gov.uk/readwriteplus/Research [accessed 10 January 2009].

DfES Standards Unit (2005) *Improving Teaching and Learning in ICT (Draft)*. London: Department for Education and Skills.

Dutton, WH and Helsper, EJ (2007) *The internet in Britain.* Oxford: Oxford Internet Institute, University of Oxford.

Excellence Gateway *Dictionary of ICT Terms* [online]. Available at: www.qiaresources4ict.net/ [accessed 10 January 2009].

Learning Skills and Improvement Service *Subject Learning Coaches programme* [online]. Available at: www.subjectlearningcoach.net/index.aspx) [accessed 10 January 2009].

8
Personal ICT skills: processes

This chapter will help you to:

- use ICT systems to meet the needs of your teaching and professional life;
- find, select and exchange information in your teaching and professional life;
- develop and present information in your teaching and professional life.

Links to minimum core ICT
B Personal ICT Skills.

     Use ICT Systems.

     Find, select and exchange information.

     Develop and present information.

Links to LLUK Professional Standards
BK2.4 Flexible delivery of learning, including open and distance learning and online learning.

BP2.4 Apply flexible and varied delivery methods as appropriate to teaching and learning practice.

BP5.1 Select and develop a range of effective resources, including appropriate use of new and emerging technologies.

CK3.5 Ways to support learners in the use of new and emerging technologies in own specialist area.

CP3.5 Make appropriate use of, and promote the benefits of new and emerging technologies.

Links to Certificate in Teaching in the Lifelong Learning Sector (CTLLS)
Unit 2 Planning and enabling learning.

Links to Diploma in Teaching in the Lifelong Learning Sector (DTLLS)
Unit 2 Planning and enabling learning.
Unit 3 Enabling learning and assessment.
Unit 4 Theories and principles for planning and enabling learning.

Introduction

Golden et al (2006) reporting on research into the use of technology by teachers in FE stated that the majority of lecturers surveyed used e-learning in their teaching. This use was focused on research, access to information and creating teaching materials and preparing lesson plans. The FE and Skills sector consists of several different areas such as FE Colleges, Adult and Community Learning (ACL), Work-Based Learning (WBL) and Offender Learning and Skills (OLAS). Each sub-sector has its own unique characteristics so that both access to technology and use of e-learning varies.

Teacher training in relation to e-learning has taken several forms. In ACL, WBL and OLAS, the e-guides programme has been available while in FE Colleges, an earlier pro-gramme centred around ILT Champions provided the initial stimulus. The Learning and Skills Improvement Service (LSIS) will be providing new training programmes across the sector from 2009 (e.g. eCPD). The LSIS Excellence Gateway gives access to the materials developed under e-guides and ILT Champions programmes.

This chapter follows the ICT personal skills identified in the ICT minimum core and focuses on the use of technology in your teaching and professional life. It identifies the skills and understanding that you will need and the ways of developing them. The mix of skills and understanding that you require is likely to vary, depending on your role and in what part of the FE sector you are working.

For example:

> Access to technical staff will be different depending on whether you are working within a college or in the community. Troubleshooting skills will need to be more advanced in a community setting, where you will often be working some distance from any technical support.

PRACTICAL TASK PRACTICAL TASK PRACTICAL TASK PRACTICAL TASK PRACTICAL TASK

Needs

Consider your role and how you will need to use ICT in your teaching and professional life. How would you assess your skills and knowledge and prioritise the areas that you would need to develop? Table 8.1 provides a structure for the assessment.

Table 8.1 provides a means of analysing your personal understanding and skills in rela-tion to the ICT minimum core. The columns Section and Key areas present the standard. In the Skills and understanding column you should indicate your current knowledge and skills and in the Activity column, those actions that could help you develop your skills in that area. The final step is to use the last column, Priority, to show how important that area is to your development.

Section	Key areas	Skills and understanding	Activity	Priority
Using ICT systems	select, interact with and use ICT systems independently to meet a variety of needs in your teaching and professional life			
	evaluate the effectiveness of the ICT systems you have used			
	manage information storage to enable efficient retrieval			
	follow and understand the need for safety and security practices, particularly in relation to risks to vulnerable learners			
	manage basic troubleshooting and know when to ask for support			
Finding, selecting and exchanging information	select and use a range of sources of information independently to meet a variety of needs in your teaching and professional life			
	access, search for, select and use ICT-based information and evaluate its fitness for purpose			
	select and use ICT to communicate and exchange information for a variety of professional and personal purposes safely, responsibly and effectively evaluate your use of ICT–based communication and exchange of information			

Table 8.1 ICT skills and knowledge analysis

Section	Key areas	Skills and understanding	Activity	Priority
Developing and presenting information	enter, develop and format information independently to suit its meaning and purpose and to meet a variety of needs in your teaching and professional life, including text and tables, images, numbers and records			
	bring together information to suit audience, content and purpose			
	present information in ways that is fit for purpose and audience			
	evaluate the selection and use of ICT tools and facilities used to present information			

Table 8.1 ICT skills and knowledge analysis

Audience

The personal skills standard places an emphasis on using technology to meet the needs of your intended audience and ensuring it is fit for purpose. Both these objectives relate to the learners that you are teaching. There are likely to be several groups with different characteristics, needs and ICT skills. It is important to consider each group so that you are able to use ICT to meet their needs.

For example:

Using ICT systems so that applications are selected which the learners are able to use or are useful for them to develop skills in.

Finding, selecting and exchanging information so that located information is suitable for the group whereby it is easy for them to read and understand and also relates to their needs.

Developing and presenting information that motivates the group.

REFLECTIVE TASK

Learners

Reflect on the characteristics of your learners and identify the ICT systems, information and content that would be most appropriate for them.

Evaluation

The standard stresses the importance of being able to evaluate your experiences, that is, being able to compare and contrast the effectiveness of undertaking tasks in different ways, perhaps using different applications. What is the most effective method? You should consider the time, cost and outcome of each approach.

Using ICT systems

This section considers the technical skills that you will need in your teaching and professional life.

Independent use

The use of ICT systems in your professional and teaching life can cover a wide range of areas. Some of the main ones are:

- Researching your subject;
- Preparing materials and activities;
- Presenting information in class;
- Supporting learners in using technology.

These cover both assisting your own productivity (e.g. word processing notes) and interacting with learners (e.g. using an electronic whiteboard). The key point is that you become an independent user, able to undertake complicated activities involving several steps to achieve a successful outcome.

The range of technology that you must be able to use independently will depend on your own role but is likely to include: communication technology (e.g. e-mail, VLEs and text messages), office applications (e.g. Microsoft Office), other applications (e.g. e-portfolios, quiz tools, online assessments, internet browsers, mind mapping and image editors) and equipment (e.g. personal computers, electronic whiteboard, scanners, printers and digital cameras).

For example – VLE

Using a VLE involves both the basics of logging on and off and also how you upload files, access communication forums, provide feedback to learners and the various other functions that are provided. The key is learning how to integrate the VLE into your teaching.

The range of technology that you need to use will depend on your own situation. Most colleges now provide a VLE, electronic whiteboards are widely available and e-portfolios are being used in some areas. However, you may want to integrate blogs, wikis or other systems into your teaching. You must make your own assessment.

Many systems can be adjusted to meet the needs of individual learners, allowing them to be more accessible. It is therefore important that you are able to understand the functionality of settings so that you can assist the learners.

Identify an ICT system that you would like to use in your teaching and prepare a learning activity based on the technology.

Evaluation

A key element in becoming an independent user of ICT is that you are able to evaluate the effectiveness of the ICT systems that you have used. This would allow you to learn from your experience and reflections. This will enable you to select the most appropriate way of achieving an outcome.

Information storage

ICT storage systems offer considerable benefits to teachers because you can save materials, examples of learners' work, research evidence and the many other items of information which will assist you in your teaching. However, simple storage is only part of the process. You need to structure your storage so that you can efficiently locate content when you need it. This requires that you understand the functions required to manage files and folders such as create, open, save, print, delete, view, rename, copy and move. It also requires an ability to develop logical folder structures and an awareness of different types of file (e.g. image files).

There are numerous storage media available, such as memory sticks and compact discs, as well as internal hard drives. It is often necessary to transport resources between locations and you must be aware of the issues and options available to you.

Folders

Consider your needs for storage of learning materials over a long period. Design and implement a folder structure for this purpose. It needs to be meaningful so that you recall the meaning of the folder names, perhaps after an interval and also flexible so you can add new content as it is needed.

Safety and security

You need to take responsibility both for your own safety and that of your learners. The learning environment may be a classroom within a college or a community location that is being used temporarily for educational purposes. In the latter situation you may have to transport and set up portable ICT equipment in the location. This will require careful consideration to create a safe environment and will involve:

- the layout of computers;
- ensuring cables do not trip people;
- ensuring equipment cannot fall on people;
- the provision of safety equipment.

Inappropriate use of technology can cause repetitive strain injury (RSI) which is often associated with using equipment in a way that puts stress on your limbs. It is therefore important to use technology correctly.

In addition to safety concerns there are many security issues associated with ICT. In terms of teaching and learning some key issues are:

- keeping your password and username secure and following your employer's procedures (e.g. regularly change the password);
- making sure that information such as learning materials, learners' work, assessment and other information are kept safe. This can be achieved through keeping copies. A network system will be centrally backed up so that any content will be safe;
- protecting the ICT system from virus or spyware infections. This is important where learners may want to transport work between their homes and college or when you are accessing learners' work at home or employment. You may also want to download materials from websites to use in your teaching. It is therefore important to understand virus protection;
- being careful not to disclose personal information or break confidentiality.

PRACTICAL TASK PRACTICAL TASK PRACTICAL TASK PRACTICAL TASK PRACTICAL TASK

Data protection

Visit the Data Protection Registrar's website and identify what the legal obligations are on your organisation to protect personal information. Identify in your own organisation who is responsible for implementing the act and what guidance is available to you.

Troubleshooting

Troubleshooting is concerned with identifying problems, solving them or asking for help if the predicament is too difficult. It covers issues such as: software freezes, understanding error messages (e.g. storage full) virus or spyware threats and printer paper jam. Many education providers have guidelines for users that limit what actions they are allowed to undertake.

For example:

A solution to some problems is to uninstall software. However, in many organisations only technicians are permitted to install or uninstall software.

In your home, the situation changes so you may need to be able to undertake this type of task.

REFLECTIVE TASK
BEELECLIAE 1V2K

Problems

Reflect on your experience of problems you have encountered and consider what skills it would be useful to develop in order to be able to solve basic difficulties.

Scenario Study – E-portfolio

The college is introducing an e-portfolio system to assess learners and to help them develop a lifelong resource of evidence about their accomplishments. Teachers are being asked to consider how they could employ the system within their classes and to familiarise themselves with the functionality of the system.

Discussion

The main functions of an e-portfolio system are:

1. To store content through uploading files of information and images to provide evidence of achievement.
2. To share evidence with other users (e.g. teachers and peers) so that they can provide feedback.
3. To select collections of evidence as part of assessment processes.
4. Some e-portfolios offer blogs and other functions.

The key is initially to explore the system in a systematic way.

Finding, selecting and exchanging information

This section considers the information skills that you will need in your teaching and professional life.

Independently selecting and using sources of information

ICT-based sources of information are important in preparing you to teach an individual class or a whole course. You must be able to independently select and use a variety of sources of information to meet your professional needs. This will involve you:

- discriminating between alternative sources of information to identify which is most suitable for your learners.
- evaluating information sources and judging if the information is fit for purpose.

There are several different ICT-based sources (e.g. websites, podcasts and blogs) in addition books and other non-ICT sources.

It is not enough to be able to judge if information is appropriate and suitable. You also need to ensure that you are free to employ it. A lot of information is covered by copyright and other legal constraints (e.g. the Data Protection Act). You have to judge if you can use the content without infringing the law. Large volumes of Open Educational Resources are now available from across the world and many universities, colleges and other sources have made their learning materials available free of charge.

PRACTICAL TASK PRACTICAL TASK PRACTICAL TASK PRACTICAL TASK PRACTICAL TASK

Open University

Visit the Open University's OpenLearn site (http://openlearn.open.ac.uk/) and browse the resources to locate content that you could use in your teaching. Find out the conditions that you need to satisfy in order to avoid infringing copyright or any other conditions.

It is important that you adequately show the sources of your materials by using citations in the appropriate way. This will serve as an example to your learners so that they avoid plagiarism which is something you also need to be able to detect.

PRACTICAL TASK PRACTICAL TASK PRACTICAL TASK PRACTICAL TASK PRACTICAL TASK

Plagiarism

Consider how plagiarism is defined in your own setting (e.g. college and awarding body). How could you detect it?

Searching for information

The world wide web is a huge information resource and in order to be able to exploit its potential you need to search it effectively using a search engine and purposeful browsing. A basic level of skill is to be able to:

- access a website by entering its address (i.e. URL) into a browser;
- navigate in and across different websites to browse for suitable information;
- use a search engine to find appropriate web pages;
- bookmark useful web pages.

Many users of search engines never go beyond entering some search terms and considering the first page of sites found. This is very limited and you should be able to use more advanced techniques to make effective use of the resource. Some advanced methods are:

- multiple search terms;
- enclosing search terms in quotation marks;
- searching within results;
- using logical operators.

It is often more effective to use multiple search terms than a single one as this is more likely to locate a better match. If you enclose your search terms in quotation marks (e.g. 'Space Fight') the search will locate pages with this phrase on them. Some search engines treat all terms in this way so it is useful to understand how the one you are using works. Many allow you to refine your search by searching within the results of your earlier search. This is effective in narrowing down a search to locate your information sources.

Logical operators allow you to develop complex search criteria by using:

- OR;
- AND;
- NOT.

which are very useful in searching the world wide web.

For example:

CPU OR memory will match any pages that display either of the terms.

CPU AND memory will match with pages that display both terms.

CPU NOT memory will match only with pages that contain the keyword CPU but which do not have the keyword memory.

In addition to searching the world wide web, you will probably also need to locate information on databases or computers. Relational operators allow you to define precise ranges of numerical criteria. They are often used in the searching of databases. They are:

- < less than;
- > more than;
- = equal to;
- <= less than or equal to;
- >= more than or equal to.

For example:

All items more than 1000 can be expressed as >1000.

Sales less than or equal to £2500 can be expressed as <= £2500.

On your own personal computer you will probably have hundreds if not thousands of files. It is important to be able to locate them. Operating systems provide search functions to find files and folders. Figure 8.1 shows the search function in the Windows XP operating system. It may also be necessary to search individual documents and so Microsoft Office applications offer the Find function to search for words or phrases.

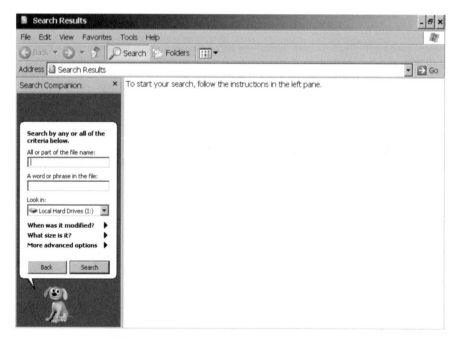

Figure 8.1 Microsoft Windows XP Search

The information displayed on a website is not always accurate or valid. Anyone can set up a website to present their views of the world. These may show the developer's prejudices and bias about a particular subject. You need to be able to evaluate sources and identify those which can provide quality information.

Some basic suggestions to evaluate a website are:

- When was the website last updated – information is often dynamic and can be rapidly out of date. A well maintained website will be regularly updated.
- Who operates the website? Are they appropriate for the information it contains?
- Who is linked to the website? The links may indicate if other people accept its content.
- Is the information accurate? Does your knowledge of the subject agree with the site?

REFLECTIVE TASK

Information

Consider your experience of finding information on the world wide web. How have you judged the accuracy and validity of the sources you have found? What lessons have you learnt?

Communication

E-mail is now a major channel of communication between teachers, within educational providers and between teachers and learners. It has the virtues of speed, informality, the ability to attach files and efficiency but it can be used irresponsibly by copying messages to individuals that the originator did not intend, sending offensive messages, provoking arguments and sending misleading messages. It is important to use e-mail efficiently and effectively by adapting the message and style of communication to meet the situation.

You must be able to use (e.g. open mailbox, create, read, reply, forward, add and open attachments) and manage (e.g. create folders and sub–folders to store messages and attachments) the e-mail system. In addition, you need the ability to create contact information and to develop mailing lists (e.g. learners in specific classes).

The educational uses of communication technology is not limited to simply sending e-mail. It also incorporates using communication forums, blogs, wikis and e-portfolios which all require the teacher to understand the nature of the communication environment.

CASE STUDY – ALICE – ONLINE FORUM

Alice is facilitating a forum for learners who are studying for a management qualification. The online group is aimed at providing the learners with some peer support outside of the face-to-face sessions. Her role is to support the group's communication by occasionally offering advice and information. She notices that there have been several e-mails exchanged between two learners that are aggressive and offensive. What is even more disturbing is that other learners appear to be joining in. What can she do?

Discussion

It is not unusual for arguments to start in communication forums. Messages are often short and informal and it is easy to misunderstand one or to feel provoked and respond in anger. This can result in more angry messages until it is out of control.

1. It is often good practice at the start of a forum to ask everyone to agree to a code of conduct (e.g. netiquette) or to develop one so that they have a sense of ownership. An important item in a list of netiquette is never to reply to a message in anger.
2. Sending aggressive or offensive messages is called flaming. To stop an argument e-mail each person involved directly and ask them to calm down and reflect on what they are doing. In other words, try to act as a peace-maker.
3. Remind everyone of the code of conduct.
4. Try to resolve the original dispute. It is often quite minor.
5. Keep calm and reduce the temperature in the forum.

Moderation needs to be light in touch but timely. It is important to visit forums regularly and to keep in touch with the discussion. Learners should know you are present but do not send too many messages. The forum is for the learners, not you.

Blogs can be used as a means of developing reflective skills. They are essentially websites that allow users to present information in date order. Other people can add comments to the information presented by the blog owner thus providing feedback. They are being used in all types of education. Wikis are specialist websites that allow a group of people to collaborate on a joint project to create a document. In education they are employed to develop collaborative and co-operative skills through a group activity. E-portfoilos are different in that they are a repository of evidence to demonstrate a person's skills, understanding and experience. However, e-portfolios also enable teachers and peers to provide feedback on the evidence. In some cases blogs, wikis and e-portfolios have been integrated together. You need to gain experience of all of these systems as they continue to grow in importance in education and training.

There are other types of ICT-based communication such as:

- Instant messenger;
- Twitter;
- Text messages.

Instant messenger is a live form of communication where several people can communicate through text messages. It is often useful as a live tutorial or for group work. Twitter is another live communication system but limited to short messages and is intended to enable allow participants to tell each other what they are doing. It is probably best at helping people learn to form groups or practise communication. Text messages are widely used by large numbers of people to communicate on the move. Its use in education is often to keep learners informed of any changes in their course (e.g. session postponed) or to remind them of deadlines.

Evaluation

It is important to review and reflect on your experiences of using communication technology. Consider factors such as the time taken, how the learners or peers responded to the application used, how effective the communication was and what alternative methods could have been used.

Developing and presenting information

This section considers the developing and presenting of information skills that you will need in your teaching and professional life.

Enter, develop and format information

This section deals with the creation of materials based on gathering information from a range of sources. It is important to be able to edit materials to make them appropriate for your learners or other groups. You must be able to use a wide range of functions including inserting, deleting, copying, cutting and pasting text and images and also techniques such as drag and drop. The aim is to be able to produce content that meets the needs of your intended audience.

For example:

Create a handout to summarise the key points of a taught session.

Edit existing worksheets to take into account changes in the curriculum.

Layout and format

The layout of a document can assist its readability and attractiveness. You need to show you can adjust layout to incorporate columns, change margins (i.e. top, bottom, left and right), add headers and footers and alter the page orientation. You might want to have a wide right hand margin so that the learners can annotate the material or to use a header to identify the material (e.g. Level 2 NVQ Business Administration). There are various reasons why you should need to adjust the layout of a document (e.g. to attract attention and improve readability).

Applications provide the tools and functions to format a document such as bullets, colour, font, character size and tables. It is important that you use them appropriately and effectively. The overuse of formatting features can produce a distracting presentation that discourages learners from using them. You should aim to employ the tools systematically for distinct purposes.

For example:

Use different fonts for headings to distinguish them from the rest of the text.

Highlight key points to make them stand out.

Use coloured text to show the relationship between different sections.

Tables are often an effective way of displaying information to show the relationships between different elements. Word processing and spreadsheets offer many functions for the construction of tables. They are also useful for presenting information.

PRACTICAL TASK PRACTICAL TASK PRACTICAL TASK PRACTICAL TASK PRACTICAL TASK

Worksheet

Create a worksheet for one of your groups of learners, using the functions available in a word processor such as Microsoft Word. Do not overuse the features but present an attractive document that would encourage learners to study it.

Learners will often initially judge the quality of learning content by its appearance so it is important to lay out and format materials to meet their needs and motivate them to use the material.

Pictures

Pictures are a useful component of education and training. There are many subjects where an image can make clear an issue or illustrate the context far more effectively than most alternatives, other than a field trip. Digital images are straightforward to capture with a digital camera and can be stored in large numbers. You can record the practical work of groups of students to provide examples for future groups and gather pictures to illustrate courses (e.g. construction, hairdressing, floristry, engineering and any subject with a practical aspect).

To make the maximum use of images, you will need to edit and manipulate them for distinct purposes. You must develop the skills of changing the size of an image, cropping pictures to concentrate on the key elements of the image, move the location of a picture and alter file formats for different purposes (e.g. smaller file size for website). There are lots of picture editing tools available and Figure 8.2 shows an image being cropped in Microsoft Office Picture Manager. This application provides the functions to manage your image collection and also perform basic picture editing.

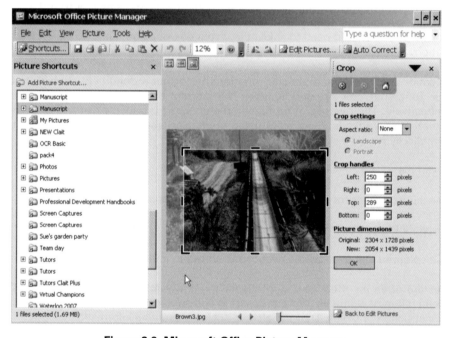

Figure 8.2 Microsoft Office Picture Manager

Numerical information

It is often necessary to present and analyse numerical information. The foundation skills required are that you can enter data and analyse it using formula and functions. Spreadsheets (e.g. Microsoft Excel) offer functions to let you perform many mathematical operations. You also need to be able to develop formulas to carry out mathematical operations. In addition to formulas and functions you have to understand referencing (i.e. absolute and relative), replication and the different types of data.

The presentation of your spreadsheet is important since it can influence your interpretation of the data. You need to be able to format the data (e.g. decimal places) as well as adjust the layout of the information by changing row and column sizes, enclosing tables in borders and changing gridlines.

A very useful function of spreadsheets such as Microsoft Excel is that you can present data in the form of graphs and charts. Microsoft Excel provides a wizard to help you create a wide variety of graphs and charts (e.g. line, column and pie charts). Figure 8.3 shows the range available. Charts and graphs are effective at presenting numerical information to learners.

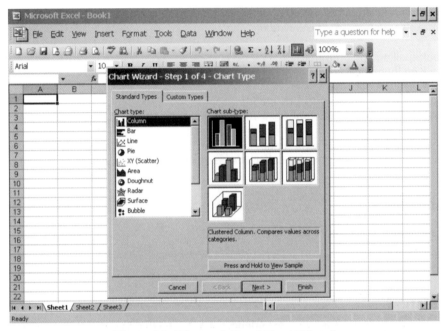

Figure 8.3 Microsoft Excel Chart Wizard

Information stored in a spreadsheet or a database can be sorted and queried to locate items that solve a problem. You may need to sort student information to identify those learners who are performing poorly so that they can be offered extra assistance.

If you are using a spreadsheet or database table you can re-order the records into ascending or descending order either alphabetically or numerically. This can often help you identify the records you need. There is also a complex sort where you use more than one criterion (e.g. age and gender of students). In addition, the filtering functions assist you in locating specific information. You need to be able to sort and filter data to solve a problem such as locating particular records.

Create

For many education and training purposes creating content is a regular task. This will often involve combining text, numerical tables and images together into a single document. Several applications (e.g. Microsoft Publisher and Word) provide the tools to integrate different types of information. The effective combination of data requires that you import them into a single document and use functions such as text boxes, text wrapping and grouping elements.

The simple task of combining of text, images and numerical data together is only the start. You must be able to edit the material and present it in an attractive way for your learners. After investing effort in producing a document, the ability to edit it to meet similar but different needs of another group is useful. These skills are required of a teacher as they will enhance your productivity.

The creation of materials is not simply a technological task; it also requires good quality control to ensure it is suitable for its purpose. A handout containing spelling mistakes will not impress students or convince them to take the material seriously. You need to undertake some basic checks including:

- check spelling and grammar;
- check mathematical calculations;
- proof read the document;
- ensure that it is consistently presented;
- provide it with a version number so you can check it is the most up-to-date copy.

Your employer may have style guides and other conventions that you need to keep to plus the subject you teach may also have ways of working (e.g. business or art worlds).

PRACTICAL TASK PRACTICAL TASK PRACTICAL TASK PRACTICAL TASK PRACTICAL TASK

Integrate images, text and numerical information

Create a document that you need combining text, pictures and numerical information together.

Evaluation

It is important to learn from your experiences. Each time that you undertake a significant task, it is wise to review the choices you made and the processes you undertook to decide if it was the best way. You should consider:

- Did the outcome meet the needs of the target group?
- How long did the task take?
- Did you achieve the desired quality?
- What functions and facilities did you employ? Would other choices have been better?
- What other factors influenced the task?

The best results are often achieved by reviewing the material during the creation process so that you can redraft or change the presentation rather than waiting until you have finished.

REFLECTIVE TASK

Creating content

Consider your experience of producing materials for teaching or another task and try to identify what you found difficult and why?

A SUMMARY OF KEY POINTS

> The majority of teachers use technology in their teaching.

> Each sub-sector of FE and Skills has its own unique characteristics so that access to technology and teacher training varies and its appropriate use also varies.

> It is important to consider the needs of each group of learners so that you can use ICT to meet their requirements.

> It is vital to evaluate your experiences. Compare and contrast the effectiveness of undertaking tasks in different ways perhaps using different applications. What is the most effective method? You should consider the time, cost and outcome of each approach.

> Use ICT systems to meet the needs of your teaching and professional life. In particular you need to develop:

 - the skills to make you an independent user;

 - an understanding of how to store information effectively;

 - an understanding of the safety and security needs of yourself and your learners;

 - the skills of identifying problems, solving them or asking for help.

> Find, select and exchange information in your teaching and professional life. In particular you need to develop:

 - the skills to independently select and use sources of information;

 - the skills of searching for information and judging its quality and suitability;

 - the ability to use communication technology.

> Develop and present information in your teaching and professional life. In particular you need to develop:

 - the skills of entering, developing and formatting information;

 - the ability to lay out and format documents;

 - the skills to manipulate and edit images;

 - the skills to enter, lay out, format and analyse numerical information;

 - the ability to create documents that integrate text, numerical information and pictures.

REFERENCES AND FURTHER READING

Clarke, A (2006) *CLAIT Plus.* London: Hodder Arnold.

Clarke, A (2007) *ICT Skill for Life.* London: Hodder Arnold.

Clarke, A (2009) *ICT Functional Skills.* London: Hodder Arnold.

Excellence Gateway (2008) [online]. Available at: http://excellence.qia.org.uk/ [accessed December 2008].

Golden, S, McCrone, T, Walker, M and Rudd, P (2006) *Impact of e-learning in Further Education: Survey of Scale and Breadth*, NFER Research Report 745. Runcorn: DIUS.

Appendix 1
Qualified Teacher Learning and Skills

Qualified Teacher Learning and Skills (QTLS) and Associate Teacher Learning and Skills (ATLS) are the qualifications required for teachers and trainers in the FE and skills sector. The FE and skills sector covers a variety of provision that provides education and training to people in FE and sixth form colleges, ACL, WBL and OLAS. It is a very wide and diverse education and training sector with links to schools, employers and higher education.

The qualification training courses are available on a part- and full-time basis and cover students with experience of teaching and those new to the profession. They provide the skills and understanding needed to work as a teacher or trainer in this diverse and complex sector. Teachers and trainers may work on a full- or part-time basis and develop the skills to meet the needs of the many different learners in this sector.

REFERENCES AND FURTHER READING REFERENCES AND FURTHER READING

1. Institute for Learning [online]. Available at: www.ifl.ac.uk/services/p_wwv_page? id=523&session_id=#whatisit [accessed 3 February 2009].
2. City and Guilds, [online]. Available at: www.cityandguilds.com/cps/rde/xchg/ cgonline/hs.xsl/qtls.html [accessed 3 February 2009].
3. Lifelong Learning UK, Sector Skills Council for Teachers and Trainer in Further and Skills sector, guidance on initial qualifications [online]. Available at: www.lluk.org/documents/uoa_generic.pdf [accessed 3 February 2009].
4. Department of Innovation, Universities and Skills, a guide to further education teacher qualifications, [online]. Available at: http://www.dius.gov.uk/publications/ guide2007no2264.pdf [accessed 3 February].
5. Learning Matters, books on QTLS and ATLS, [online]. Available at: www.learningmatters.co.uk/ [accessed 3 February 2009].
6. University and College Union, initial Teacher Training and Continuing Professional Development in the Learning and Skills Sector: an update [online]. Available at: www.ucu.org.uk/media/pdf/8/c/itt_cpd_dec06.pdf [accessed 3 February 2009].
7. OCR awarding body, OCR Teaching in the Lifelong Learning Sector Qualifications, [online] available at: www.ocr.org.uk/Data/publications/support_materials/VRQ_TLLS_L3_L4_Award_L3_L 4_Cert_L5_Dip_SM_Presentation.ppt [accessed 3 February 2009].
8. Edexcel awarding body, QTLS qualifications [online]. available at: developments.edexcel.org.uk/tlls/qual/ [accessed 2 April 2009].

Appendix 2
Minimum core

In 2004, a minimum core of skills and knowledge was defined for teacher training programmes in the FE and skills sector. It covered literacy, language and numeracy. Its intention was to assist teachers and trainers to be able to support learners who had literacy, language or numeracy learning needs who were studying any subject. It would therefore provide an inclusive approach to skills for life by providing any teacher with sufficient skills and understanding to assist the learner.

In 2007, a new framework for teacher training qualifications was launched for the FE and skills sector. In response to the new framework, a revised minimum core was introduced for literacy, language and numeracy but with the addition of a minimum core for ICT. The latter was included since ICT alongside the other subjects had been declared a skill for life. That is, a subject that was fundamental to living and working in a modern society.

REFERENCES AND FURTHER READING REFERENCES AND FURTHER READING

The Sector Skills Council for lifelong learning Addressing literacy, language, numeracy and ICT needs in education and training: Defining the minimum core of teachers' knowledge, understanding and personal skills A guide for initial teacher education programmes, June 2007 [online]. Available at: www.lluk.org/documents/minimum_core_may_2007_3rd.pdf [accessed 3 February 2009].

Appendix 3
Skills audit and action plan

The ICT minimum core covers a wide range of skills and understanding. It is important to be able to assess your own strengths and weaknesses and develop an action plan to address the gaps. In Chapters 1, 7 and 8 tables in the form of checklists are provided to help you identify gaps in your understanding of the issues or personal skills. The three tables are:

- Table 1.1 ICT minimum core analysis
- Table 7.1 ICT communication skills analysis
- Table 8.1 ICT skills and knowledge analysis

An action plan requires not only the skills and knowledge you need to improve but also the timescales over which the development will take place and how you are going to undertake the improvements. The plan below is an example showing the types of information and action you need to take. It can develop your own layout to meet your own preferences. It is always important to plan to reflect on the activity not least to decide if it achieved your objective but also to consider how to build on the experience.

Action plan

Objective	Dates	Activity	Reflections of success	Next steps
To gain a better understanding of social disadvantage and its impact on learning	By June 2009	To read a range of reports and other publications on social disadvantage	Although I have improved my understanding of the general nature of social disadvantage and learning I am not sure how that translates into actions that I can take	I will arrange to visit the local authority community college to discuss their approaches to supporting socially disadvantaged learners

Appendix 4
Development

ICT is a fast changing and developing field in which it is important to maintain and enhance your skills and understanding continuously. In order to plan and monitor your own progress it is important to maintain records of your development. These can be useful evidence in demonstrating that you are meeting the CPD requirements of a teacher or trainer in the FE and skills sector. They are also a way of helping you to reflect on your experiences and activities in order to deepen your learning and help you identify your next steps.

Professional development record

Date	Activity	What did I learn?	What should I do now?	Next steps
13 February 2009	I attended a conference of the use of wikis in education and training and was able to take part in a group activity	It is quite daunting to edit another person's input and difficult to be objective when another person changes your own efforts	I need to participate in more wiki activities to understand how to use the technology most effectively	Contact the college's e-learning manager
27 March 2009	I have been reading the *Delivering Digital Inclusion*, the Government's action plan to address the digital divide	A large amount of detail about the nature of social disadvantage and ICT	I need to gain an understanding of practical activities that I could integrate into my classes to help learners develop ICT skills	Speak to one of the ICT Skill for Life tutors

Personal blog – reflection

An important part of any professional development is reflection. This is the means of gaining the maximum benefit from an activity or experience. There are many ways of recording your reflection but one that is increasingly being used is a blog. This is a web-site that is organised so that messages can be added in date order rather like a diary.

A blog can be entirely personal in that no one else has access or a completely public one in which the whole world can read your messages and send comments. These are the extremes and many people choose a middle position in which peers and colleagues have access but no one else. This allows you to gain the benefits of colleagues' comments and advice on your reflections. This can be very valuable.

E-portfolio

It is important to keep records of your professional development. This is not simply because it is required but also since it represents your own efforts and achievements. There are many times during a professional lifetime when you will need to explain your experience. An e-portfolio provides the means to store and organise evidence of your activities, training, experience and achievements.

If you are a member of the Institute for Learning then you will have access to the Reflect e-portfolio. However, many employers are now providing portfolios for staff and students. You should explore the options and decide what is best for you. A key consideration is that an e-portfolio is a long-term investment so you need to know whether your access will be guaranteed for a lifetime or if it is straightforward to move your content to a new location.

Appendix 5
ICT minimum core checklist

LLUK (2007) *Addressing Literacy, Language, Numeracy and ICT Needs in Education and Training: Defining the Minimum Core of Teachers' Knowledge, Understanding and Personal Skills*. London: Lifelong Learning UK.

Chapter	Element	Notes
Chapter 2 Different factors affecting the acquisition and development of ICT skills	aware of a range of personal and social factors including: attitudes in the wider society, age, motivation, gender, socio-economic status, ethnicity and disability or learning difficulty that affect the acquisition and development of ICT skills	
	able to reflect on your own and learners' attitudes and attainment, with regard to personal use and new learning that involves ICT	
	aware of ICT research in the acquisition and development of ICT skills	
Chapter 3 Importance of ICT in enabling users to participate in public life, society and the modern economy	the importance of ICT in enabling users to participate in and gain access to society	
	the importance of ICT in enabling users to participate in and gain access to the modern economy	
Chapter 4 Main learning disabilities and difficulties relating to ICT learning and skills development	aware of the impact that learning difficulties and disabilities, as described in *Delivering Skills for Life: Introducing Access for All*, can have on ICT learning	
	aware of the resources, specialist equipment, teaching strategies and referral procedures which can help learners overcome their difficulties in ICT use and learning	

Chapter	Element	Notes
Chapter 5 Potential barriers that inhibit ICT skills development	to be aware of personal factors that may inhibit the development of ICT skills	
	to be aware of the institutional factors that may inhibit the development of ICT skills	
	to be aware of the teaching and learning factors that may inhibit the development of ICT skills	
Chapter 6 Communicating about ICT	be aware of methods and purposes of assessment in ICT	
	be aware of the role of communication in ICT	
	be aware of effective ways to communicate	
	understand what is meant by purposeful use of ICT	
	understand the essential characteristics of ICT	
	be aware of the ways learners develop ICT skills	
Chapter 7 Personal ICT skills: communication	to communicate with/about ICT in a manner that supports open discussion	
	to be able to assess your own, and others' understanding	
	to be able to recognise differences in language needs; formulate and provide appropriate responses and recognise appropriate use of communication about/with ICT by others	
	to be able to use language and other forms of representation	
Chapter 8 Personal ICT skills: processes	use ICT systems to meet the needs of your teaching and professional life	
	find, select and exchange information in your teaching and professional life	
	develop and present information in your teaching and professional life	

Glossary

This section provides an explanation of the terms used in relation to ICT.

Adobe Acrobat – a file format (.pdf) used to distribute documents on the internet.

Assistive technology – equipment and alternative methods that assist disabled people to use ICT.

Asynchronous – communication that does not need the users to be online at the same time as each other.

Back up – to keep a copy of your files safe to avoid the loss of information.

Blended learning – combining traditional teaching methods with e-learning to get the best of both approaches.

Blogs – a blog is a website in which participants reflect on a subject. The entries are provided in date order and people can add comments to other entries.

Bulletin Board – an online website at which you post, receive and reply to messages.

Chat – online communication using synchronous text.

Collaborative learning – learning as a group.

Conferencing – a means of supporting group discussion online.

Courseware – e-learning materials, modules and courses.

Creative Commons – a copyright licence that gives users a degree of freedom.

E-learning – the use of technology to support, deliver and enhance learning.

E-portfolios – an electronic portfolio is an online system that allows the learner to collect and store evidence of their learning. Evidence can be in any format (e.g. multimedia) and can be organised for assessment or other purposes.

Flame – an angry or offensive e-mail message.

File Transfer Protocol (FTP) – a way of transporting files over the internet.

Firewall – a security system to protect a computer system.

Forum – an online site in which learners can discuss and collaborate.

ILT (Information and Learning Technology) – an alternative term for e-learning.

Learning object – a discrete piece of e-learning material.

Lurking – reading and benefitting from online discussion forums while not contributing.

M-learning – using mobile devices to support and deliver learning.

Moderator – supporter and manager of an e-mail or other form of discussion forum.

Multicasting – a way of broadcasting content across the internet.

Netiquette – principles to control the behaviour of online forums.

Online learning – delivering and supporting learning through the internet.

Open Educational Resources – free learning materials that are available online.

Podcast – an audio recording that can be distributed online.

Portal – a website that organises links to many other sites and resources.

RSS – Real Simple Syndication is a distribution mechanism for podcasts, blogs and other content.

Screen Reader – an application that reads aloud any text that is displayed on a screen.

Search engine – an application which allows you to search the world wide web for information.

Streaming – a technique that allows video and audio to be sent to you quickly.

Synchronous – communication that requires the users to be online at the same time.

Thread – a group of e-mail messages linked to a particular theme in an online forum.

Twitter – an online communication method that allows short messages to be sent.

Virtual Learning Environment (VLE) – an online resource that allows learning materials, forums and other resources to be organised to support learners.

Vodcast – the video version of a podcast (i.e. distributing video material online).

W3C – the organisation which sets accessibility standards for the world wide web.

Webquest – an online exercise based on using information on a range of websites.

Wikis – a wiki is a website or online area in which a group of people can create and edit a joint document.

Web 2.0 – a group of technologies that assist users of the world wide web to create content.

ZIP/UNZIP – a way of compressing large files format to make it easier to send through communication technology.

Index